KETO COOKING *for* HEALING *and* WEIGHT LOSS

VIVICA MENEGAZ, Author of 1,001 Paleo Recipes

PAGE STREET
PUBLISHING CO.

PAGE STREET
PUBLISHING CO.

First published in 2021 by

Page Street Publishing Co.

27 Congress Street, Suite 105

Salem, MA 01970

www.pagestreetpublishing.com

Distributed by Macmillan, sales in Canada by The Canadian Manda Group.

25   24   23   22   21   1   2   3   4   5

ISBN-13: 978-1-64567-261-6

ISBN-10: 1-64567-261-1

Library of Congress Control Number: 2020942956

Cover and book design by Kylie Alexander for Page Street Publishing Co.

Photography by Yasmin Alishav

Printed and bound in China

THIS BOOK IS DEDICATED TO ALL THE PEOPLE WHO BELIEVE IN THE BODY'S INTELLIGENCE AND ABILITY TO HEAL ITSELF.

CONTENTS

INTRODUCTION

"If you do not take time for your health today, you will have to take time for your illness tomorrow."

—DR. BRUCE BOND

Born into an Italian restaurateur family and having spent my first twenty years immersed in Italy's food culture, it was only natural that I developed a passion for food from an early age.

Outside of Italy, Italians are famous for two things: their love of football and their love of food. On this basis, I am wholeheartedly an Italian because of the latter.

Years ago, I expressed my passion for food through my love of food photography. As I began to question the food I was photographing, this passion evolved and deepened as I came to understand more about how my personal food choices were impacting my health.

As someone who has always been holistically minded, I turn to natural health solutions first. Eventually this led me to my true heart's vocation: nutrition and helping people heal using food as a tool.

I made my first connection to nutrition thanks to the help of my first mentor, Dr. Deborah Penner. She actively pushed me to pursue my interest in nutrition, recommended courses of study and eventually employed me as her patient advocate.

It was during the years I worked for her that I had my first encounter with the ketogenic diet. Back in 2014, few people were talking about the ketogenic diet outside of the realm of epileptic seizure control. Tracing back to the 1920s and '30s, the ketogenic diet's first therapeutic application was in controlling what were considered at the time to be untreatable seizures. In the 1990s, the ketogenic diet was brought back to the public's attention by bodybuilders who utilized it to maximize fat loss while sparing lean muscle mass.

When I started recommending the ketogenic diet for weight loss and health in Dr. Penner's nutrition practice, only a handful of people, such as Jimmy Moore and Maria Emmerich, were writing and talking about it. There were few resources I could refer to for recipes, information and personal life experiences with this approach.

Much to my shock and disbelief, I had just been diagnosed as a prediabetic. It was at this point I flipped the mirror and used my personal challenge as fuel for my research into the ketogenic diet. Slowly my focus changed from the local, sustainable Paleo diet I was recommending, and I started to incorporate more of the ketogenic ratios that helped me control my blood sugar and hormonal issues. Paleo is the ideal foundation for a healthy diet, and I found that the proper macronutrient ratios take it to the next level.

I realized that this way of eating could be the solution for all the serious metabolic issues I saw in my patients, and myself, and that it could be the most valuable tool not just for weight loss, but for healing. The metabolic system is deeply connected to the endocrine system, and one of the biggest mistakes of most weight-loss diets is that they completely ignore the health of both, in the quest to shed pounds.

A very common misconception I come across every day with my readers and prospective clients is that they think losing weight will lead them to better health. It is actually the opposite. **Forcing the body to lose weight indiscriminately, without first addressing underlying issues of why the weight gain occurred in the first place, will just cause further damage.** Sometimes the damage done to the metabolism by years of low-fat, low-calorie and yo-yo dieting takes concerted effort to correct, and even then, the damage may be beyond repair!

The good news is, there is a solution, and not just for your stubborn weight problem! We aren't talking about another quick-fix diet that comes at the price of your health and well-being. This is a long-term lifestyle change that will provide you with plenty of delectable food options, give you freedom from hunger and unchain you from your sugar cravings. It's a lifestyle that supports your vibrant health (mental and physical!) and your quality of life. Welcome to a therapeutic ketogenic diet!

KETO AND WHY TO DO IT

IS THIS YOU?

Your morning alarm rings. You've had another restless seven hours of sleep. Ignoring the beeping alarm, you turn over for just five more minutes. Those five minutes turn into half an hour and suddenly, you're running late. In the frenzy of getting ready, you have no time to eat breakfast. Thank goodness for coffee.

The day passes in a frenzy of sugar highs and lows. You spend your morning in scattered bouts of productivity. Your willpower has gone out the door by lunchtime, and an unfocused mind leads you to spend your lunch break chowing down a sandwich at your desk. In a desperate attempt to regain your energy, you reach for more caffeine and sugar.

Then comes the mid-afternoon slump. You feel your energy tanking and the sugar cravings hit hard. Thankfully you keep those candy bars in your bottom drawer!

After another long day, you return home and find yourself too tired to cook. You had grand plans of going to the gym, but instead, you find yourself parked on the couch with some takeout in hand, pizza being the food of choice this particular night. Soon enough, the whole box is empty and you don't even remember eating the last piece. Those sneaky food gremlins! You're too tired to even clean up, and with drippings of guilt weighing on you, eventually you find yourself drifting to sleep with the promise lingering on your mind that tomorrow will be better.

. . . Only to rinse and repeat the next day.

Reflecting on your past, you've noticed the same patterns crop up. Diet after diet, you always trend toward low-fat and low-calorie because isn't that the way you're supposed to lose weight? You've been told this your whole life!

The results of each diet are always short-lived. And the worst part is actually the poor energy levels, the grumpy moods, the insatiable hunger and the embarrassing digestive issues.

Maybe you've caught wind of these "new" or "renewed" low-carb diets, namely the Atkins and the conventional ketogenic diets. These were supposed to be the diets to end all diets. And they were! For a whole few weeks. After the initial weight loss, you plateaued and then your hair started falling out, your sleep became irregular and so the story continues.

To your stress and fatigue, we can add a number of health conditions you might be experiencing, such as prediabetes, type 2 diabetes, hypothyroidism, adrenal fatigue, autoimmune diseases or hormone imbalances, which only makes things worse.

Whether you're living with one of these diagnoses or not, you know the truth. At the root of it all, you know you are not eating well. You desperately want to shed a few (or many) pounds and to look and feel healthier. But you are so tired, busy and overwhelmed!

HOW DID YOU GET THERE?

We were taught from a young age about the (not-so) trusty food pyramid. Right at the bottom, forming the basis of your diet, you were told to eat all the carbohydrates. First, there were the "healthier" versions like bread, pasta, cereals, whole grains and rice. As industrialized food set in, the pizza, cake, candy and soda drinks also crept into our diets. Whole foods were pushed out and above all else, fat was slowly being removed.

Fat has become the twenty-first century villain. Over time, our carbohydrate-heavy diet has filled with more processed sugars than our bodies know what to do with. As a result, our waistlines have blown up and lifestyle-induced diseases have increased. Maybe you were one of the many who adopted the attitude that so long as you kept your fat intake low, you would get a clearance by the doctor come checkup time.

You used margarine instead of butter. You opted for the chicken breast over the drumsticks. You politely asked for your salad dressing on the side. You swapped your full-fat products for low-fat ones with promises of a slimmer waistline. And so long as you occasionally ate some fruits, vegetables and plenty of grains, you were walking down the path to perfect health. Or so you thought.

Sadly, the carbohydrates we are dependent on for the majority of our modern diet are doing us more harm than good. In reality, the human body is not designed for such high carbohydrate consumption. Our metabolism is not so far removed from our ancestors, let alone from our own grandparents. We haven't evolved away from whole foods. Nor have we evolved toward processed foods.

Statistics prove that U.S. adult consumption of added sugars has increased by more than 30 percent over the last three decades (Source: The Obesity Society, 2014, www.obesity.org/news/press-releases/US-adult). This does not include the rest of our daily carbohydrate consumption of "healthy" carbs. At the end of digestion, processed or not, your body treats carbohydrates in the same way. Only the addition of fats or fiber may slow down the process but only marginally so. When your cells are constantly bombarded with more carbs (code word for sugar) than they are able to immediately utilize, your body needs to constantly release insulin in order to direct that sugar into storage (as fat!).

Think of insulin as your personal traffic controller. It sees a surge of carbs storming through, madly honking their horns. If your body does not immediately make use of this surge of carb traffic, in an effort to avoid congestion, it's insulin's job to redirect this unused energy to a place where it can be stored (such as in your fat cells).

Unfortunately, when this pattern has been on repeat for years and years, your body develops a system of accumulating fat as a way to store those excess sugar calories. And because your body can't deal with carbs without insulin's help, you need to employ more and more traffic controllers (insulin) to expedite the process. As a side effect of the constant insulin release, your cells become insensitive to it, requiring higher and higher quantities to do the job. Your cells are being overworked and underpaid. Oh no . . . sounds like a union strike waiting to happen.

With your body unable to use the excess sugar in your system, and your cells unable to keep up with the growing traffic problems, your blood sugar levels start to rise. The sugars aren't being redirected effectively. It's like someone's left the keys in the ignition and hooligans have taken off on a high-speed joyride down the highway. When this happens many times over, it's utter chaos! No wonder you feel those sugar highs and consequent crashes.

Insulin is the hormone controlling fat storage, and when this system is thrown out of control, you get fatter! Leptin, the satiety hormone, is also connected to insulin. As your leptin signals start to fade, you become leptin resistant and are less able to feel satisfied after a meal, throwing off your hunger signals.

When all this happens, your blood sugar bounces up and down every time you eat sugar, leading to reactive hypoglycemia and constant hunger and cravings. Of most importance, your blood sugar will remain elevated when your cells become insulin resistant. Your pancreas is responsible for releasing insulin and when overburdened, will not be able to keep up with the production of insulin. This is when type 2 diabetes may become your reality.

These sugar and hormone imbalances act as stressors, taxing your adrenals even more. And this is on top of external daily stressors like work deadlines, paying bills, crying babies, relationship issues and so forth! Consequently, an endocrine domino effect ensues, which usually ends up in thyroid dysfunction.

SO HOW DO WE FIX THIS COMPLEX SCENARIO?

In reality, there is no magic bullet solution, as we might often be led to believe.

A complex problem requires a multifaceted solution. Every individual presents a unique set of problems and health issues. Think about it this way: It's taken you years to get into this mess, and it may take some time to get you out of it.

If you go to a doctor or a dietitian, they will most likely suggest some version of the same way of eating that created the problems in the first place. That's if you are lucky. Otherwise you will be put on medications, which are just going to mask the symptoms, but never fix the problem.

How do I address this problem in my nutrition practice? First and foremost, changes in diet and lifestyle are needed. Sometimes adequate supplementation can assist.

To build or rebuild the desired strong base of health, my number one tool is food! As wise people said before, food is medicine, and that is why I use a therapeutic ketogenic diet.

ABOUT A THERAPEUTIC KETOGENIC DIET

So, what is a therapeutic ketogenic diet?

By definition, a ketogenic diet is a way of eating with the purpose to induce nutritional ketosis by restricting carbohydrate intake and balancing daily amounts of fat and protein.

Ketosis is a metabolic state induced by the restriction or elimination of carbohydrates, in which the body starts burning ketones as the main source of energy. Ketones are small energy-containing substances, similar to glucose in structure, but derived from fatty acids.

During the process of "Keto adaptation" (restricting carbohydrates for a minimum of three weeks), the body gradually switches to maximum fat-burning ability through a series of physiological changes. Some of those changes enable the brain to switch from burning glucose to burning ketones and allow the muscle to burn free fatty acids, reserving ketones for the brain. Keto adaptation also protects the body from using lean muscle protein as a source of energy. This is why bodybuilders find it so appealing. You get maximum fat burn with minimum loss of muscle.

WHY IS KETOSIS DESIRABLE TO YOU?

Aside from the maximum fat-burning and muscle-sparing effects, ketosis has a series of additional benefits. It:

- Provides a long-term, steady energy source that removes hypoglycemia-induced hunger and cravings
- Stabilizes blood sugar thereby reducing stress to the body (especially the adrenals)
- Provides a steady, optimal source of fuel to the brain, eliminating brain-fog
- Improves insulin sensitivity (reducing the risk of diabetes)
- Reduces inflammation
- Eliminates candida
- Stops feeding glucose-hungry cancer cells
- Reduces symptoms of menopause

Ketosis can normally be achieved by restricting carbohydrates under 20 grams per day, but you might be able to tolerate up to 40 to 50 grams and remain in ketosis. This all depends on your degree of carbohydrate tolerance. Protein is usually kept at around 25 percent of the macronutrients unless you are very active.

You may be wondering how this is different than a typical Keto diet.

This approach is a way of eating based on the principles of a Paleolithic diet that uses a ketogenic ratio of macronutrients. This can be summarized as eating Paleo foods while restricting carbohydrates.

Now you may be asking the question, what are Paleo-approved foods and what are the benefits of eating a Paleo diet?

A Paleo diet is a way of eating that mimics the way our hunter–gatherer ancestors were eating, at least in theory. In my practice, eating Paleo means avoiding all processed foods, grains, legumes and dairy. Please note, eggs are not dairy (there is always some confusion over this!). Dairy is classified as any milk-based product, like cheese, yogurt, cream and milk.

Here are some of the benefits of a Paleo diet. It:

- Reduces toxic load (general improvement of all health conditions)
- Avoids most common food allergens (again, improving most conditions)
- Provides a nutrient-rich diet
- Is rich in plant enzymes
- Is rich in high-quality animal protein
- Is good for you, and good for the environment, because you are eating organic foods that are not genetically altered and are sustainably sourced

Over the years, I've encountered many more health benefits of eating this way, including those of a Paleo diet. It:

- Supports endocrine health by providing vital nutrients and eliminating stressors
- Gradually reduces or eliminates allergies
- Improves general immune function, which means less infections and colds
- Greatly increases energy
- Eliminates menopause symptoms and generally helps rebalance hormones

LET'S KEEP IT SIMPLE!

The bottom line is, you want a long-term, simple solution that delivers results without going crazy over the details. You want a way of eating that fits a busy lifestyle, and supports your health and well-being, while keeping you satisfied and free of cravings.

These were my goals in creating this cookbook. This book contains my many years of knowledge and experience from working in the field of nutrition. I have found great success in eating this way, both personally and with my clients.

I've already done the hard work to keep it simple for you, so you can achieve your goals!

WHY IS THIS BOOK DIFFERENT?

This is not your typical ketogenic cookbook. In fact, it is quite different.

You will not find recipes loaded with cheese, cream and bacon. I've deliberately avoided creating recipes that rely on processed or prepackaged ingredients because I don't believe this is the most health-supporting way to eat.

What you will find is a lot of great-tasting foods that might remind you of times past, of the way your grandmother used to cook. This will be especially true if she came from a Mediterranean country like I did!

The reason why this book is different is simple. I combine all of the best ingredients, focusing on nutrient density, to promote a healthy body and sustainable, healthy weight loss.

Every recipe was studied not only for ketogenic macronutrient ratios, but also for maximum healing power! All of the ingredients are fresh and organic, so they contain valuable vitamins and nutrients. These living foods contain enzymes vital for proper digestion and assimilation, so you do not have to take them in a pill. They also contain many important phytonutrients, with multiple health benefits—some of which have not even been fully discovered.

These nutrient-dense foods, combined in the right ratios of low carbohydrate, moderate protein and high fat, and in simple, delicious recipes, will create the foundation for your long-term health and wellness moving forward.

A NOTE ABOUT INGREDIENTS

I do not specify the term "organic" in front of every ingredient. I use (and recommend that you use) all organic ingredients and pasture-raised meats as part of your Keto Paleo lifestyle.

I acknowledge that in many cases organic ingredients are more expensive than conventional ones. But there are a few things I want to help you understand when considering the benefits of investing in good food to support your long-term health:

- Pesticides and herbicides are not only toxic for bugs and weeds, but also for you and our planet. A clean body, free of toxins, is a foundational element of nutrition and a pillar of health.

- Conventional meats are produced in feedlots, with complete disregard to animal welfare. This is not just an ethical concern, but also a matter of avoiding feeding your body with the stress hormones of the meat you consume.

- Toxin accumulation from nonorganic foods and feedlot meats can lead to cancer, autoimmune diseases and a series of degenerative diseases.

- Genetically modified plants suppress biodiversity. The very life-supporting system we (and planet Earth) rely on relies on biodiversity to thrive.

- Organic ingredients are of superior quality. They contain more nutrients and taste much better.

- Supporting a more sustainable system in turn supports you and your health!

I think it is important to make a stand for organic foods for several reasons.

In some instances, you may think the price of local and organic food to be unreasonably inflated. When you consider the bigger picture and the investment in your long-term health, it helps to put this premium into perspective.

If you are living on a budget, what are your priorities? Why are we, as a society, so quick to upgrade to the latest technology, and spend money on expensive clothes and dining out, and yet so shocked at the idea of spending more on quality food at home?

More often than not, we go straight to the grocery budget with a red pen to slash our expenses when we should first turn to other areas of our lives. After all, great-tasting and nourishing food is what supports our health. This is what fuels our bodies and our lives! We should treat our health with the same respect as we treat our gadgets and designer dresses.

It may help to make a list of your monthly expenses and actually look at how much you are spending on food in comparison to other items in your life. Are there subscription services, fancy gadgets, takeout meals, daily lattes or other unnecessary amenities you can cut back on before you look at downgrading the quality of your grocery items? From my experience, I've found cutting out processed and packaged foods frees up money to spend on higher quality fresh foods. You don't need to buy expensive, well-marketed "superfoods" to be healthy. We're talking the simple and basic vegetables and meats here.

To get the most out of your organic dollars, I recommend shopping at local farmers' markets first. You can go directly to the local farmer for meats and buy a whole or half animal to save money. Buying in bulk may result in a higher upfront expense, but the long-term savings really add up! In some instances, you save up to half the price on single cuts.

If the meat is too expensive, you can always join a co-op or food-buying group or ask for a Costco membership for your next birthday. Over recent years, I've noticed Costco is starting to offer a larger variety of organic products and foods. A note of warning: Always read ingredient labels when buying manufactured products. Just because something is labeled "organic," does not always mean it is healthy . . . especially Keto Paleo healthy!

ABOUT MEAL PLANNING

Buying in bulk and cooking most of your meals in batches saves money, time and energy. It just requires a little planning. Once you get into the groove of things, it will become the new normal.

I usually grocery shop and cook on Sundays. My routine is to clean the fridge and compost or dispose of old foods in the morning. Then I make a morning of attending the farmers' market and the grocery store. When I get home, I cook a few large meat or fish recipes that will last me several days. I prefer to make my vegetables fresh on the spot. This is why my side dish recipes are all fairly quick and simple.

Meat and fish can easily be divided into portions and refrigerated, making it easier for portion control and meal organization.

MAIN MEALS

The main course forms the centerpiece of your diet! I've created an abundance of flavorful Keto main dishes you will be proud to share with family and friends. A protein in the form of meats or fish creates the basis of these main meals, and they are always accompanied with plenty of healthy fats.

I suggest that if you are on a budget, invest in organic meat before other ingredients. Because of the concept of bioaccumulation, through which toxins accumulate in animal tissues over time, meat can contain the most toxins when not sourced organically.

BUTTER POACHED SCALLOPS WITH MEYER LEMON GREMOLATA

This recipe is a great one if you want to impress your guests with your fancy ketogenic cooking! The gremolata adds a burst of fresh, bright flavor that beautifully complements the buttery scallops. Rich in protein and healthy fats, as well as iodine, this recipe will help you build strong thyroid health.

YIELD: 4 servings
PREPARATION TIME: 20 minutes

GREMOLATA

1 cup (110 g) coarsely chopped almonds

3 tbsp (45 ml) olive oil

1 clove garlic, pressed

½ cup (30 g) fresh parsley, finely chopped

1 Meyer lemon, zested

½ tsp unrefined sea salt

½ tsp black pepper

SCALLOPS

1 cup (229 g) butter

16 large scallops

¼ tsp unrefined sea salt

Preheat the oven's broiler. In a small bowl, combine the almonds, olive oil, garlic, parsley, lemon zest and salt and pepper. Mix well. Spread on a small cookie sheet and place under the broiler until browned, for about 3 minutes. Remove from the oven and set aside.

In a saucepan large enough to accommodate all the scallops side by side, melt the butter over very low heat. Once melted, add the scallops in one layer, then sprinkle with the salt. Cook just until they turn opaque, about a minute, then turn and cook for another minute, until they are cooked through. Remove the scallops from the butter with a slotted spoon. Don't overcook the scallops or they will become dry and rubbery.

Serve the scallops over a salad or over Easy Cauliflower Rice (page 103), sprinkled with 3 to 4 tablespoons (8 to 10 g) of gremolata.

NUTRITIONAL VALUES:

Total Calories:	Total Carbs:	Fat:	Protein:	Fiber:	Net Carbs:
1631 kcal	53 g	30.75 g	95 g	18 g	35 g
Per portion	Per portion	Per portion	Per portion	Per portion	Per portion
407.7	13.25	7.7	23.75	4.5	8.7

CASHEW CRUSTED SALMON WITH "PONZU" SAUCE

This recipe will impress your family! This dish is easy, super quick to make and full of flavor and healing qualities. You will love the sweetness of coconut aminos, combined with tangy lime juice, to brighten the soft round flavors of the fish and nuts. This Keto version of ponzu sauce is soy and sugar free.

YIELD: 4 servings
PREPARATION TIME: 15 minutes

1 cup (55 g) cashew pieces

½ cup (8 g) fresh cilantro, coarsely chopped

2 tbsp (28 g) coconut oil, divided

¼ tsp unrefined sea salt

1 lb (454 g) salmon fillets, with skin

3 tbsp (45 ml) coconut aminos

1 lime, juiced

In a food processor, blend the cashews, cilantro, 1 tablespoon (14 g) of coconut oil and salt, until even, green crumbles are formed.

In a medium nonstick skillet, heat the remaining 1 tablespoon (14 g) of coconut oil over high heat, then place the salmon fillets in the pan, skin side down. Immediately spread the cashew crumbles on top of the fillets, pressing them down onto the fish and creating a crust about ½ to ¾ inch (1 to 2 cm) thick. Cover immediately with a tight-fitting lid and lower the heat to medium. Cook until the salmon is turning opaque all over, about 5 minutes, then turn off the heat and let sit for another minute.

While the salmon is cooking, make the ponzu sauce by mixing the coconut aminos with the lime juice.

Serve hot with a couple of tablespoons (30 ml) of ponzu sauce on top of the salmon. This is great with Salt and Pepper Asparagus (page 115) on the side.

NUTRITIONAL VALUES:

Total Calories:	Total Carbs:	Fat:	Protein:	Fiber:	Net Carbs:
1803 kcal	42 g	98 g	127 g	5 g	37 g
Per portion 450.7	Per portion 10.5	Per portion 24.5	Per portion 31.7	Per portion 1.2	Per portion 9.2

CHICKEN CABBAGE POT PIE

Mmhhh comfort food! This is an easy ketogenic version of the classic pot pie. With a satisfying crumbly topping and a hot and creamy center, this dish will brighten any cold day.

YIELD: 10 servings
PREPARATION TIME: 60 minutes

1½ cups (168 g) coconut flour, divided

1½ cups (150 g) fine blanched almond flour

2 tbsp (8 g) fresh parsley, finely chopped

3 tbsp (12 g) fresh thyme, finely chopped, divided

1 tsp unrefined sea salt

½ cup (115 g) plus 4 tbsp (56 g) butter, plus extra for greasing

½ cup (106 g) coconut oil

1 lb (454 g) cooked chicken meat (dark meat is better)

4 cups (1 L) chicken broth

1 lb (454 g) savoy cabbage, cut in 1-inch (2.5-cm) pieces

5 oz (142 g) shallots, thinly sliced

1 tbsp (15 ml) lemon juice

½ cup (120 g) coconut cream

Preheat the oven to 350°F (177°C).

To prepare the crust, put 1 cup (112 g) of coconut flour, almond flour, parsley, 1 tablespoon (4 g) of thyme, salt, ½ cup (115 g) of butter and coconut oil in a food processor, and process on high until the dough starts to form a ball. Remove the dough from the processor, shape into a rectangle and wrap in plastic wrap before placing in the refrigerator for at least 20 minutes.

Grease a 9 x 12-inch (23 x 30-cm) ovenproof dish with butter, then place the chicken in it. In a medium saucepan, boil the chicken broth, then add the cabbage, cooking until just tender, about 3 minutes. Drain the cabbage and add it to the oven dish with the chicken, reserving the broth for later.

In a heavy-bottomed skillet, melt the 4 tablespoons (56 g) of butter over very low heat. Add the shallots and 2 tablespoons (8 g) of thyme to the butter and cook until the shallots are tender and transparent, about 5 minutes. Next, add ½ cup (56 g) of coconut flour and cook, stirring for about a minute. Add the lemon juice and stir for few more seconds, then add the coconut cream and the broth from the cabbage. Cook over high heat until the sauce thickens, stirring constantly, about 2 minutes.

Pour the sauce onto the chicken and cabbage and mix well.

Roll out the dough onto a piece of parchment paper; shape into a 10 x 13-inch (25 x 33-cm) rectangle.

Using the parchment paper, place the dough onto the baking dish, and tuck around the contents of the pan, covering the filling well on every side. Cut about 6 slits in the dough to let the steam escape.

Bake for 25 minutes, until the top is brown and sauce is bubbling. Remove from the oven and let sit for about 10 minutes before serving.

NUTRITIONAL VALUES:

Total Calories: 3285 kcal	Total Carbs: 101 g	Fat: 309 g	Protein: 52 g	Fiber: 52 g	Net Carbs: 48 g
Per portion 328.5	Per portion 10	Per portion 30.9	Per portion 5.2	Per portion 5.2	Per portion 4.8

GARLIC LEMON THYME ROCKFISH

Rockfish can be a bit bland, so adding fresh herbs and lemon gives it needed zest. I like to use ingredients that add lots of nutrients and medicinal proprieties to your diet, like cilantro and garlic. I also try to combine oven batches to save energy and time. This easy baked fish recipe can be combined as a piggyback onto anything else you are baking!

YIELD: 4 servings
PREPARATION TIME: 20 minutes

1 lb (454 g) rockfish or Alaskan cod

½ cup (120 ml) Keto Paleo Mayo (page 151)

3 cloves garlic, pressed

1 tsp fresh thyme leaves

1 lemon, zested

½ tsp unrefined sea salt

¼ tsp freshly ground black pepper

Preheat the oven's broiler. Place the fish fillets in a shallow oven-safe dish. In a small bowl, combine the mayo, garlic, thyme, lemon zest, salt and pepper and mix well with a fork. With a pastry brush or a fork, spread half the mixture on one side of the fish, then turn the fillets over, and brush with the rest of the mixture. Put the fish under the broiler for about 8 minutes, until it is just done inside and getting opaque and flaky. Do not overcook.

NUTRITIONAL VALUES:

Total Calories:	Total Carbs:	Fat:	Protein:	Fiber:	Net Carbs:
1784 kcal	4 g	144 g	103 g	0 g	4 g
Per portion	Per portion	Per portion	Per portion	Per portion	Per portion
446	1	36	25.7	0	1

HOMEMADE CHICKEN SAUSAGE

I try to limit the amount of pork I eat because it contains toxins and seems to hinder weight loss, so I wanted to have a good alternative for my breakfast sausage. This is a great, easy recipe for tasty sausage you can make at home. Enjoy all the great flavor of a hearty, robust sausage!

YIELD: 10 patties
PREPARATION TIME: 30 minutes

½ cup (118 ml) dry white wine

1 tsp unrefined sea salt

½ tsp black pepper

2 cloves garlic, pressed

1 tsp fennel seeds, crushed

½ tsp nutmeg

½ tsp allspice

½ tsp paprika

¼ tsp cayenne

1 lb (453 g) lean ground chicken

½ lb (227 g) pork, beef or lamb fat, very finely chopped

Butter or ghee, for cooking

In a large bowl, blend the white wine with the salt, pepper, garlic, fennel, nutmeg, allspice, paprika and cayenne, stirring well.

Add the meat and fat to the bowl and mix by hand until all ingredients are evenly distributed. Alternatively, you can use a mixer. Once the sausage mixture is well combined, form into ¼ cup (55 g) balls, then flatten to about ½ inch (1 cm) thick. Refrigerate overnight before cooking, to blend flavors.

When ready to cook, melt a tablespoon (14 g) of butter over high heat in a nonstick skillet. Cook the patties until browned on top and done all the way through, turning once, about 3 to 5 minutes per side.

NOTE: The sausage can be shaped into patties or cylinders, depending on how you want to use it. You can also make a double or triple batch of this sausage and freeze the patties on a baking sheet. Once frozen, transfer to an airtight freezer bag or container for ease of storage and freeze for up to a month.

NUTRITIONAL VALUES:

Total Calories:	Total Carbs:	Fat:	Protein:	Fiber:	Net Carbs:
2243 kcal	9 g	187 g	97 g	2 g	7 g
Per portion 224.3	Per portion 0.9	Per portion 18	Per portion 9.7	Per portion 0.2	Per portion 0.7

INSTANT BOLOGNESE SAUCE

This is one of my favorite pasta sauces! Usually a hearty, smooth Bolognese takes hours to prepare, and as we do not always have that much time to dedicate to a dish, I created this quick version to fit a busy lifestyle. It has all the richness of flavor of the original recipe.

YIELD: 6 servings
PREPARATION TIME: 15 minutes

3½ oz (98 g) pancetta or bacon, finely chopped

1 lb (454 g) skirt steak, or any cut of steak that's not too lean

2 medium tomatoes, finely chopped

¼ tsp fresh thyme leaves

¼ tsp sage leaves

⅛ tsp ground nutmeg

¼ cup (60 ml) red wine

½ tsp unrefined sea salt

Pinch of black pepper

1 tbsp (14 g) butter

In a heavy-bottomed or cast-iron pan, sauté the pancetta over medium heat until it starts to brown, about 3 minutes. While that's cooking, cut the steak into ¼-inch (6-mm) pieces.

Remove the pancetta from the pan, raise the heat to high and sauté the steak in the drippings until almost cooked through, about 2 minutes. Add the pancetta back to the pan, add the tomatoes, thyme, sage, nutmeg, wine, salt and pepper, and cook, stirring often, for about 5 minutes. Turn off the heat and add the butter. Stir until melted.

Serve on top of All-Purpose Keto Noodles (page 129), Easy Cauliflower Rice (page 103) or shirataki noodles (commonly found in any health food store or health food section of a commercial grocery store).

NUTRITIONAL VALUES:

Total Calories:	Total Carbs:	Fat:	Protein:	Fiber:	Net Carbs:
1813 kcal	10 g	130 g	123 g	2 g	8 g
Per portion	Per portion	Per portion	Per portion	Per portion	Per portion
302	1.6	21.6	20.5	0	1.3

KETO SLOW COOKER JAMBALAYA ON CAULI RICE

This surprisingly flavorful dish is so easy to make! Deliciously smoky and rich, it has the same texture as the classic dish. You will not be able to tell this is not the original jambalaya.

YIELD: 6 servings
PREPARATION TIME: 10 minutes + 6 hours

½ tsp sweet paprika

½ tsp dried oregano

½ tsp ground black pepper

½ tsp dried basil

½ tsp cayenne pepper

½ tsp dried onion powder

½ tsp dried garlic powder

½ tsp dried thyme

1 tbsp (15 g) unrefined sea salt

4 oz (112 g) guanciale or bacon, cut into small pieces

1 andouille sausage, sliced

½ medium onion, finely chopped

2 ribs celery

4 cloves garlic, finely chopped

3 oz (84 g) fresh tomato, chopped

1 cup (240 ml) chicken or beef broth

6 oz (170 g) chicken, cut into ½-inch (1-cm) cubes

1 lb (454 g) fresh raw shrimp, peeled

2 cups (120 g) riced cauliflower

½ cup (30 g) fresh parsley, finely chopped

Mix the paprika, oregano, black pepper, basil, cayenne pepper, onion powder, garlic powder, thyme and salt and set aside.

In a slow cooker, set on high, put the guanciale and sausage on the bottom, then add the onion, celery, garlic, tomato and broth. Sprinkle half of the seasoning over the slow cooker ingredients.

While the slow cooker mixture cooks, sprinkle the other half of the seasoning mixture on the chicken. Place the chicken in the refrigerator for 3 hours, then take it out and bring to room temperature. At the same time, bring the shrimp to room temperature as well.

After the slow cooker mixture has cooked for about 4 hours, add the chicken, shrimp and riced cauliflower to the slow cooker, stirring everything together, and cook for another hour and a half. Make sure all of the meats are thoroughly cooked, but not overcooked; they should be tender and juicy and the flavors well blended. Mix in fresh parsley just before serving. If the mixture is too watery, cook for an additional half hour with an open lid, stirring occasionally.

Serve hot.

NUTRITIONAL VALUES:

Total Calories:	Total Carbs:	Fat:	Protein:	Fiber:	Net Carbs:
1588 kcal	43 g	101 g	134 g	12 g	31 g
Per portion 264.6	Per portion 7.1	Per portion 16.8	Per portion 22.3	Per portion 2	Per portion 5.1

KETO LAMB KOFTAS

Do you love Mediterranean foods? I do, and love that special flavor that
comes from fresh spices and garlic.

YIELD: 9 meatballs
PREPARATION TIME: 20 minutes

1 lb (454 g) minced lamb, the
fattier the better

2 cloves garlic, pressed

1 lemon, zested

2 small dried peperoncino or
1 dried red serrano pepper,
crushed

1 tsp ground coriander

1 tsp ground cumin

1 tsp dried thyme

1 tsp unrefined sea salt, divided

½ tsp freshly ground black pepper

3 tbsp (45 ml) olive oil

½ cup (120 g) coconut cream

3 tbsp (45 g) tahini

3 tbsp (45 ml) freshly squeezed
lemon juice

Bring the lamb to room temperature. Place the meat in a medium
bowl, then add the garlic, lemon zest, peppers, coriander, cumin,
thyme, ½ teaspoon salt and pepper. Mix well with a spoon or with wet
hands (to prevent mix from sticking). Form the lamb into 9 flat patties.

In a large nonstick skillet, heat the olive oil over high heat until hot but
not smoking. You can test the temperature with a tiny piece of meat
to see if it sizzles.

Place the 9 koftas in the skillet and cook over high heat for about
3 minutes on each side if you like them still pink in the middle, or
4 minutes each side for well done.

While the koftas cook, mix the coconut cream, tahini, lemon juice
and ½ teaspoon salt in a medium bowl. Mix well, until they form a
smooth cream.

Serve immediately with the sauce drizzled over the koftas. They
pair nicely with a basic green salad or a parsley salad.

NOTE: You can prepare the sauce ahead and keep it at room
temperature if you will be using within a couple of hours. If making it
in advance, refrigerate it for up to a week. Bring to room temperature
to soften before using.

NUTRITIONAL VALUES:

Total Calories:	Total Carbs:	Fat:	Protein:	Fiber:	Net Carbs:
2321 kcal	20 g	207 g	92 g	6 g	14 g
Per portion	Per portion	Per portion	Per portion	Per portion	Per portion
257.8	2.2	23	10.2	0.6	1.5

LARD CRUST MEAT PIE

A savory meat pie is a great recipe you can make ahead and bring to work for lunch, or put in your child's lunchbox. It also makes a great weekend dish that will impress your family!

YIELD: 10 servings   PREPARATION TIME: 1 hour, 30 minutes

2 cups (192 g) almond flour

1 cup (112 g) coconut flour

1½ tsp (8 g) unrefined sea salt, divided

1 cup (205 g) lard, cold

1 egg

2 tbsp (28 g) butter

10 oz (283 g) shallots, finely sliced

1 clove garlic, finely chopped

2 cups (120 g) riced cauliflower

1 lb (454 g) ground beef

½ tsp black pepper

½ tsp ground cinnamon

½ tsp ground cloves

¼ tsp ground nutmeg

½ cup (118 ml) beef broth

Preheat the oven to 350°F (177°C). Grease a 9-inch (23-cm) pie dish.

In a food processor, mix the two flours and 1 teaspoon of salt until well blended, then add the lard and process until fine crumbles form. Add the egg to the processor and keep mixing until the dough is fully blended and starts to form a ball. Remove the dough from the processor and form into two balls, one slightly larger than the other. Wrap the dough in parchment paper and place in a glass dish before refrigerating for at least 15 minutes.

While the dough chills, prepare the filling. In a large nonstick skillet, melt the butter over low heat and add the shallots and garlic. Sauté until the shallots are cooked and translucent, about 3 minutes, then add the cauliflower and raise the heat to high. Sauté, stirring often, until the cauliflower is browned and tender, about 5 minutes.

In a separate large skillet, brown the beef over high heat, about 5 minutes. Add the cauliflower mix to the beef, then add ½ teaspoon salt, pepper, cinnamon, cloves, nutmeg and broth, and mix well to blend evenly. Cook until the liquid reduces to about half, about 3 minutes. Set aside to cool.

Remove the dough from the refrigerator, and place the larger ball between two large pieces of parchment or wax paper. With a rolling pin, roll out the dough evenly, until it forms a disk large enough to cover your pie dish. Repeat the process with the smaller ball to create a lid for the pie.

Peel off the top paper from the larger disk and invert the crust into the greased pie dish. Press the dough to form an even bottom crust for the pie. Add the cooked filling. Peel off the paper from the other disk, and carefully place it on top of the pie filling. Squeeze the edges of the crust together, then cut four slits in the top crust, so steam can escape. Cover the edges of the pie with strips of aluminum foil, so they will not burn.

Bake until the top of the pie is nicely browned, about 1 hour. Let cool for about 15 minutes before serving.

NUTRITIONAL VALUES:

Total Calories:	Total Carbs:	Fat:	Protein:	Fiber:	Net Carbs:
5653 kcal	259 g	437 g	211 g	136 g	123 g
Per portion	Per portion	Per portion	Per portion	Per portion	Per portion
565.3	25	43	21	13	12

PERUVIAN HERBED CHICKEN

I fell in love with this dish the first time I visited Peru. Easy and fragrant, with the flavors of cilantro and garlic, it is high in minerals and protein. This is a perfect healing food that will keep you satiated and content.

YIELD: 4 portions
PREPARATION TIME: 40 minutes

2 tbsp (28 g) coconut oil

1 tbsp (15 ml) olive oil

2 cloves garlic, finely chopped

1 lb (454 g) chicken thighs with skin, bone in

½ cup (8 g) fresh cilantro, finely chopped

½ cup (30 g) fresh parsley, finely chopped

½ tsp unrefined sea salt

1 cup (240 ml) water

In a medium-sized heavy-bottomed saucepan, heat the coconut and olive oils over medium heat. Add the garlic and cook until fragrant, about 1 minute, being careful not to burn.

Add the chicken and sauté until slightly browned, about 1 minute. Add the cilantro, parsley and salt and stir together well. Add the water and cover with a tight-fitting lid.

Cook until the chicken is fully done, and the sauce has reduced to a thick paste, about 30 minutes. Make sure the bottom does not burn, by stirring occasionally and lowering the heat if necessary.

NUTRITIONAL VALUES:

Total Calories:	Total Carbs:	Fat:	Protein:	Fiber:	Net Carbs:
1046 kcal	12 g	88 g	60 g	7 g	5 g
Per portion	Per portion	Per portion	Per portion	Per portion	Per portion
261.5	3	22	15	1.7	1.2

SLOW COOKER KOREAN SHORT RIBS

I just love Korean food! Rich with garlic and sweet flavors, it's the ultimate "umami." This recipe is an easy one that does not need any specialty ingredients, so it's accessible and a good introduction to the flavors of Korea. It is a wonderful comfort dish and pairs great with cauliflower rice.

YIELD: 8 servings
PREPARATION TIME: 10 minutes + 7 hours

4 lb (1.8 kg) short ribs, bone in

2 tbsp (24 g) LAKANTO® or erythritol (see page 168)

½ cup (118 ml) coconut aminos (see Note)

½ cup (118 ml) dry white wine

3 tbsp (45 ml) toasted sesame oil

3 cloves garlic

1 sweet onion, peeled and cut in chunks

2-inch (5-cm) piece fresh ginger, peeled

1 cup (240 ml) water

Soak the ribs in a bowl of cold water for at least 1 hour.

In a food processor, mix the LAKANTO®, coconut aminos, white wine, sesame oil, garlic, onion and ginger, until a smooth puree forms.

Place the ribs in the slow cooker and cover with the sauce and the water. Cook on high for 4 hours, then uncover the slow cooker and cook for 2 more hours on low, until the meat is very tender and the sauce has thickened.

Serve hot over Easy Cauliflower Rice (page 103).

NOTE: Coconut aminos are a great soy-free substitution for soy sauce. Find them in most health food stores or on the Internet.

NUTRITIONAL VALUES:

Total Calories:	Total Carbs:	Fat:	Protein:	Fiber:	Net Carbs:
1684 kcal	20 g	131 g	103 g	2 g	18 g
Per portion	Per portion	Per portion	Per portion	Per portion	Per portion
210.5	2.5	16.3	12.8	0	2.25

PROSCIUTTO-WRAPPED ROCKFISH

I love prosciutto because in Italy, I grew up on it. True Prosciutto di Parma is one of the healthiest preserved meats you can buy as it only uses two ingredients: pork and salt. The nice layer of fat on the prosciutto really works for a ketogenic diet, while the flavor and saltiness enhance the taste of the fish. Add butter to it all and you have a ketogenic masterpiece!

YIELD: 4 servings
PREPARATION TIME: 15 minutes

4 (4 oz [112 g]) rockfish fillets (see Note)

½ tsp unrefined sea salt

¼ tsp black pepper

5 small sprigs fresh rosemary, divided

4 large, thin slices prosciutto

4 tbsp (56 g) butter, softened, divided

Preheat the oven to 400°F (204°C).

Sprinkle the fillets with salt and pepper. Place a sprig of rosemary on each of the fillets, then wrap them each individually in a prosciutto slice. Grease a 6 x 10–inch (15 x 25–cm) baking dish with some of the butter, then carefully place the wrapped fillets in the dish. Bake until the fish is white and flaky, about 15 to 20 minutes.

While the fish cooks, melt the remaining butter in a small saucepan with the remaining sprig of rosemary on very low flame, until the butter begins to brown, about 2 minutes.

Serve the fish immediately, drizzled with some of the rosemary butter.

This recipe pairs great with Dandelion Salad with Balsamic Pancetta Dressing (page 109) or Brown-Butter Salad (page 102).

NOTE: This recipe will work with any kind of firm white fish, such as cod or halibut.

NUTRITIONAL VALUES:

Total Calories:	Total Carbs:	Fat:	Protein:	Fiber:	Net Carbs:
1063 kcal	1 g	60 g	112 g	0 g	1 g
Per portion	Per portion	Per portion	Per portion	Per portion	Per portion
265.7	0	15	28	0	0

SEARED SKIRT STEAK WITH BRAZILIAN "VINAGRETE"

You will love this easy dish and the vinaigrette, or "vinagrete," as they say in Brazil, which includes some powerful healing ingredients, like pepper, onion and cilantro. These ingredients help to remove heavy metals from the body and provide a good source of fat with the medium-chain triglyceride (MCT) oil. The meat provides much-needed raw protein, if you leave it rare in the middle. Raw meat provides essential amino acids in their intact state, which makes them easily absorbable.

YIELD: 4 servings
PREPARATION TIME: 40 minutes

½ cup (8 g) fresh cilantro, finely chopped

½ cup (75 g) onion, finely chopped

½ cup (100 g) tomato, finely chopped

½ serrano pepper, finely chopped

1 clove garlic, pressed

1 lime, juiced

½ tsp unrefined sea salt

¼ tsp freshly ground black pepper

2 tbsp (30 ml) MCT oil (see page 168)

1 tbsp (15 ml) vinegar

1½ lb (681 g) skirt steak

4 tbsp (60 g) coarse sea salt or kosher salt

Mix the cilantro, onion, tomato, serrano pepper, garlic, lime juice, unrefined sea salt, black pepper, MCT oil and vinegar in a medium bowl and set aside.

Place the meat on a plate and sprinkle with the coarse salt on both sides. Do not rub the salt in or it will be too salty. Let sit for 30 minutes, so it soaks up the salt and comes to room temperature.

Heat a cast-iron grill pan over high heat, until very hot. Sear the steak on the grill pan for about 3 minutes per side, until medium rare.

Remove the steak from the grill pan, shaking off the excess salt, and place on a warm plate. Cover and let rest for about 10 minutes.

Slice the steak in thin slices against the grain of the meat. Serve immediately with the vinaigrette on the side.

NOTE: The vinaigrette can be made up to a day ahead. Refrigerate until ready to use.

NUTRITIONAL VALUES:

	Total Calories:	Total Carbs:	Fat:	Protein:	Fiber:	Net Carbs:
	2123 kcal	26 g	148 g	162 g	2 g	24 g
	Per portion	Per portion	Per portion	Per portion	Per portion	Per portion
	530.7	6.5	37	40.5	0	6

SLOW COOKER INDIAN BUTTER CHICKEN

This dish is medicinal, uses the properties of a great number of spices, is full of nutrients and has all the right macronutrient ratios!

YIELD: 6 servings   PREPARATION TIME: 3 hours

2 lb (908 g) boneless chicken meat, thighs preferred, cut in large chunks

1 tbsp (15 ml) fresh lime juice

1 tsp unrefined sea salt

1 tsp red chili powder

6 cloves

10 peppercorns

1-inch (2.5-cm) cinnamon stick

2 bay leaves

2 tbsp (5 g) fenugreek leaves

10 almonds

¼ tsp cardamom seeds

1 cup (250 g) thick coconut yogurt

1 tsp coriander powder

1 tsp cumin powder

1 tsp turmeric powder

3 tbsp (42 g) coconut oil

1 onion, finely chopped

2 tsp (19 g) garlic paste

1 tsp ginger paste

2 cups (473 ml) chicken stock

5 oz (142 g) fresh ripe tomatoes, pureed

4 tbsp (56 g) butter, cut in small chunks, softened

In a large bowl, mix the chicken with the lime juice, salt and red chili powder. Cover and marinate for at least 1 hour.

In a nonstick or cast-iron skillet over medium heat, gently roast the cloves, peppercorns, cinnamon, bay and fenugreek leaves, almonds and cardamom seeds, stirring often until they darken, about 3 minutes.

Let the spice mixture cool, then grind in a clean dry coffee grinder, until they turn into a fine powder. Mix this spice powder with the coconut yogurt, the coriander, and the cumin and turmeric powders and add them to the marinating chicken. Mix well and let sit for another hour.

Heat the coconut oil in a Dutch oven or heavy-bottomed saucepan over medium heat. Add the onion and cook stirring often until browned, about 5 minutes. Add the garlic and ginger pastes, and cook for another minute, stirring. Raise the heat to high and add the marinated chicken, after dripping off most of the liquid. Reserve the marinade.

Quickly stir the chicken over the highest heat, until it is heat sealed on all sides. Add the chicken stock, tomato puree and chicken marinade to the pan. Lower the heat to medium and cook until the chicken is tender and the sauce is reduced to about half, about 30 minutes. When the chicken is ready, turn off the heat and mix the butter into the sauce. Let sit for 5 minutes and serve with Keto Naan Bread (page 136).

NUTRITIONAL VALUES:

Total Calories:	Total Carbs:	Fat:	Protein:	Fiber:	Net Carbs:
2342 kcal	39 g	186 g	172 g	18 g	21 g
Per portion	Per portion	Per portion	Per portion	Per portion	Per portion
390.3	6.5	31	28.6	3	3.5

SPAGHETTI ALLA SICULA

Noodles Sicilian style! This is one of the most truly Italian recipes I can think of . . . although of course I had to change it up just a bit to fit our Keto lifestyle. I've removed the grains and added good fiber. You'll be surprised by just how much flavor it has!

YIELD: 4 servings
PREPARATION TIME: 10 minutes

4 servings All-Purpose Keto Noodles (page 129)

4 tbsp (60 ml) extra virgin olive oil

4 tbsp (15 g) fresh parsley, finely chopped

2 cloves garlic, finely chopped

1 peperoncino, chopped

Prepare the noodles as indicated in the recipe, keeping warm.

In a nonstick skillet, heat the olive oil over low heat, then add the parsley, garlic and peperoncino. Sauté for about 2 minutes, until the garlic is golden but not burnt, or it will turn bitter.

Add the noodles to the pan and mix gently with the sauce, for about 30 seconds. Serve immediately.

NUTRITIONAL VALUES:

Total Calories:	Total Carbs:	Fat:	Protein:	Fiber:	Net Carbs:
1083 kcal	59 g	75 g	43 g	51 g	8 g
Per portion	Per portion	Per portion	Per portion	Per portion	Per portion
270.75	14.5	18.7	10.7	12.75	2

STUFFED CHICKEN THIGHS WITH MACADAMIA PESTO

It's amazing how fast and easy it is to create delicious foods! You will be amazed by this tasty recipe, and its rich, nutty yet fresh flavor. This is a great source of fat and protein. I bet your kids will like it too!

YIELD: 4 servings
PREPARATION TIME: 10 minutes

3 oz (84 g) macadamia nuts

½ cup (8 g) chopped basil

3 tbsp (45 ml) olive oil

2 tbsp (30 ml) MCT or coconut oil (see page 168)

2 cloves garlic

½ tsp sea salt

4 boneless chicken thighs, about 4 oz (112 g) each

Preheat the oven to 350°F (177°C).

Add the macadamia nuts, basil, olive oil, MCT or coconut oil, garlic and salt to a small food processor. Mix on the high setting until a coarse paste is formed.

Wash the chicken thighs and pat them dry; lay them flat, inside up in a glass oven pan. Place about 2 tablespoons (30 g) of the macadamia pesto filling on each chicken thigh. Fold the thighs closed, then spread the leftover pesto on top.

Bake for 30 minutes. When the thighs are done, place them under the broiler over high heat for 5 minutes to brown the top.

NUTRITIONAL VALUES:

Total Calories:	Total Carbs:	Fat:	Protein:	Fiber:	Net Carbs:
1502 kcal	14 g	124 g	96 g	7 g	7 g
Per portion	Per portion	Per portion	Per portion	Per portion	Per portion
375.5	3.5	31	24	1.7	1.7

STUFFED VEGETABLES WITH BEEF

This is a classic recipe straight from my childhood. The subtle flavor of nutmeg blends beautifully with the heartiness of the beef and the fresh note of the vegetables.

YIELD: 6 servings
PREPARATION TIME: 25 minutes + 45 minutes

1 lb (454 g) ground beef

2 medium tomatoes

1 tsp unrefined sea salt, plus a pinch, divided

2 small bell peppers

2 medium zucchini

1 small yellow onion

3 tbsp (45 ml) melted butter, plus more for greasing, divided

1 clove garlic, pressed through a garlic press

1 egg

⅓ cup (37 g) coconut flour

½ tsp freshly ground black pepper

½ tsp nutmeg

Preheat the oven to 350°F (177°C) and bring the ground beef to room temperature.

Cut the tomatoes in half to create two half "cups." Scoop out the inside of the tomatoes with a spoon. Sprinkle the insides of the tomatoes with a pinch of salt and lay upside down on a plate to drain.

Cut the bell peppers in half and remove the seeds.

Cut the zucchini in half lengthwise and scoop out the flesh with a small pointed spoon, to create little boats.

Peel the onion and cut it in half, then separate the individual layers so they are like cups. If the bottom of any of the onion cups has a hole, cut a slice of onion layer to patch it.

Grease 2 large ovenproof dishes with butter and place all the vegetable cups in them.

In a large bowl, combine the ground beef, garlic, egg, coconut flour, 1 teaspoon of salt, black pepper and nutmeg. Mix well, with your hands or a spoon, until well blended. Pour the melted butter over the mix and stir to incorporate. The mix should be soft but not runny.

Fill the vegetable cups with the meat mixture, distributing it evenly.

Bake for 45 minutes to 1 hour, depending on the size of the vegetables and desired doneness.

Serve immediately, with a salad. This dish can be also eaten cold.

NUTRITIONAL VALUES:

Total Calories:	Total Carbs:	Fat:	Protein:	Fiber:	Net Carbs:
1999 kcal	124 g	123 g	126 g	59 g	65 g
Per portion 333	Per portion 20	Per portion 20.5	Per portion 21	Per portion 9.8	Per portion 10.8

THAI GREEN CHICKEN CURRY

Have you ever had a fresh curry made from scratch? This green curry will blow
your taste buds away with the sharp, green, spicy flavor! You can make the green curry paste a
day or two ahead and refrigerate it in an airtight container.

YIELD: 6 servings   PREPARATION TIME: 30 minutes

2 small Thai chilies or 1 serrano
pepper

1 medium shallot, coarsely
chopped (¼ cup [13 g])

4 cloves garlic

2-inch (5-cm) piece fresh ginger,
peeled and cut in pieces

1 stalk fresh lemongrass, sliced or
3 tbsp (45 g) lemongrass paste

½ tsp ground coriander

½ tsp ground cumin

1 tbsp (10 g) dried shrimp meal
(see Note)

1 cup (16 g) fresh cilantro, roughly
chopped

⅓ cup (14 g) fresh basil leaves

½ tsp ground white pepper

3 tbsp (45 ml) fish sauce

1 tbsp (12 g) LAKANTO® or
erythritol (see page 168)

1 tbsp (15 ml) lime juice

3 tbsp (42 g) coconut oil

1 lb (454 g) boneless chicken thighs, cut in large chunks

1 (13.5 oz [400 ml]) can full-fat coconut milk

1 lime, zested

Place the chilies, shallot, garlic, ginger, lemongrass, coriander, cumin,
shrimp meal, cilantro, basil, white pepper, fish sauce, LAKANTO® and lime
juice in a food processor and mix until a smooth paste is formed. Set aside.

In a large, heavy-bottomed skillet or a wok, melt the coconut oil over
high heat. When the oil is hot, add the chicken and quickly brown on
the outside, for about 2 minutes.

Remove the chicken from the pan and set aside. Add the curry paste
to the pan and quickly stir-fry for about 1 minute, then add the coconut
milk and the chicken to the pan. Bring to a slow simmer, then reduce
the heat to low and cover. Cook until the chicken is fully done, stirring
occasionally, about 8 to 10 minutes. Add the lime zest and stir well.
Serve immediately on Easy Cauliflower Rice (page 103) or with Keto
Naan Bread (page 136).

NOTE: Shrimp meal is available in the Hispanic food section of
supermarkets; as with the lemongrass paste, read the ingredients—it
should only contain dried shrimp.

NUTRITIONAL VALUES:

Total Calories:	Total Carbs:	Fat:	Protein:	Fiber:	Net Carbs:
1471 kcal	32 g	103 g	111 g	8 g	24 g
Per portion	Per portion	Per portion	Per portion	Per portion	Per portion
245	5.3	17.1	18.5	1.3	4

THAI MEATBALLS

As a big fan of Thai food, this is one of my favorite recipes ever! I love how simple and convenient it is, and that it is a bit different from the usual meatballs. I make a large batch and then refrigerate them for few days of quick meals.

YIELD: 8 portions (2 meatballs per portion)
PREPARATION TIME: 45 minutes

1 tbsp (14 g) coconut oil

1 lb (454 g) ground beef, at room temperature

2 tbsp (30 g) Red Curry Paste (page 152)

⅔ cup (160 g) coconut cream

2 eggs, at room temperature

½ tsp unrefined sea salt

Preheat the oven to 350°F (177°C). Grease a cookie sheet with the coconut oil.

In a large bowl, mix the beef, curry paste, coconut cream, eggs and salt. Form 16 little meatballs from the mixture. Place the meatballs on the cookie sheet and bake until fully cooked but still soft and juicy, about 30 minutes. You can turn the meatballs after 20 minutes, so they brown on both sides.

NOTE: You can also fry the meatballs in a nonstick skillet with coconut oil. Cook until they are just pink inside, about 4 to 5 minutes.

NUTRITIONAL VALUES:

Total Calories:	Total Carbs:	Fat:	Protein:	Fiber:	Net Carbs:
1684 kcal	20 g	131 g	103 g	2 g	18 g
Per portion	Per portion	Per portion	Per portion	Per portion	Per portion
210.5	2.5	16.3	12.8	0	2.3

MOLE TURKEY MEATBALLS

Mole made from scratch is usually a complicated affair. I tried to simplify the original Mole Poblano recipe while preserving the complex, rich flavors.

YIELD: 7 portions (4 meatballs per portion)   PREPARATION TIME: 50 minutes

3 tbsp (45 ml) melted coconut oil, divided

1½ lb (681 g) ground turkey

3 tbsp (45 ml) bacon drippings

1 egg

½ cup (50 g) almond meal

¼ tsp cayenne pepper

¼ tsp smoked paprika

1 tsp unrefined sea salt, divided

1 cup (150 g) onion, chopped

1 tsp ground cumin

1 tsp ground coriander

1 tsp ground cinnamon

2 cloves garlic, pressed

2 dried ancho chilies, stemmed and seeded, cut into thin strips

5 cups (1.25 L) chicken stock

½ cup (100 g) chopped ripe tomato

2 tbsp (24 g) erythritol (see page 168)

4 tbsp (36 g) finely chopped almonds

2 (½ x 2-inch [1 x 5-cm]) orange rind strips

1 oz (28 g) unsweetened baking chocolate

Preheat the oven to 400°F (204°C). Oil a large cookie sheet with 1 tablespoon (15 ml) of coconut oil.

In a large bowl, mix the ground turkey with the bacon drippings, egg, almond meal, cayenne pepper, paprika, sea salt and 1 tablespoon (15 ml) of coconut oil. Using a spoon, form meatballs about 2 inches (5 cm) in diameter, and place them on the cookie sheet. You should get about 28 meatballs. Bake the meatballs for about 10 minutes, then turn off the oven and let them sit until the sauce is ready.

Heat the remaining 1 tablespoon (15 ml) of coconut oil in a large Dutch oven over medium heat. Add the onion and cook until tender, about 5 minutes.

Add the cumin, coriander and cinnamon to the onion and continue cooking, stirring often for another minute. Add the garlic and the chilies and cook another 2 or 3 minutes, until the chilies soften.

Add the chicken stock, tomato, sweetener, almonds and orange rind and stir. Continue cooking for another 10 minutes, stirring often. Add the chocolate to the sauce and stir until melted.

Puree the sauce, either with an immersion blender or by pouring into a glass blender. Blend until the sauce forms a smooth puree.

Lower the heat to low and add the meatballs and the sauce to the Dutch oven and mix gently to coat with sauce. Cook on low for another 10 minutes. Serve with Easy Cauliflower Rice (page 103).

NUTRITIONAL VALUES:

Total Calories:	Total Carbs:	Fat:	Protein:	Fiber:	Net Carbs:
1762 kcal	31 g	99 g	187 g	15 g	16 g
Per portion	Per portion	Per portion	Per portion	Per portion	Per portion
251	4.4	14.1	26.7	2.1	2.2

TURMERIC FISH CURRY

This is a quick and easy dry curry with all fresh ingredients. You will be amazed by the burst of warm flavors of ginger and turmeric! These fresh roots contain great anti-inflammatory properties.

YIELD: 4 servings
PREPARATION TIME: 25 minutes

2 oz (56 g) shallots, sliced fine

3 tbsp (42 g) coconut oil, divided

3-inch (7-cm) piece fresh turmeric root, finely grated

1-inch (2.5-cm) piece fresh ginger, finely grated

1 fresh serrano pepper, seeded and finely chopped

1 clove garlic, pressed through a garlic press

1 lb (454 g) rockfish, striped bass or red snapper fillets, cut in 2-inch (5-cm) pieces

¼ tsp unrefined sea salt

In a large nonstick skillet, sauté the shallots in 2 tablespoons (28 g) of coconut oil over a very low flame, until they are transparent, about 5 minutes.

Increase the heat to medium, add the turmeric, ginger, pepper and garlic to the skillet and sauté for about 3 minutes, stirring often.

Remove the mixture from the skillet, and put it on a plate.

Add the remaining tablespoon (14 g) of coconut oil to the skillet and raise the heat to high. When the oil is hot add the fish and cook for about 3 minutes, flip, then add the spice mixture and the salt and lower the heat to medium.

Cook, constantly stirring, until the fish is cooked through, about 5 minutes.

Serve immediately with a salad or shirataki noodles.

NUTRITIONAL VALUES:

Total Calories: 840 kcal	Total Carbs: 14 g	Fat: 43 g	Protein: 82 g	Fiber: 3 g	Net Carbs: 11 g
Per portion 210	Per portion 3.5	Per portion 10.7	Per portion 20.5	Per portion 0	Per portion 2.7

BREAKFAST

Conventional diets often proclaim that breakfast is the most important meal of the day. While I agree, where many diets get it wrong is by recommending fruit and grains. The reason breakfast is important is it should set you up with a more regulated blood sugar level to start your day, but it depends on what you eat! Just as you can set yourself up for success, likewise, you can set yourself up for a blood sugar rollercoaster.

My rule for breakfast is simple: Savory is better than sweet. Any sweet flavor, even in the form of an artificial sweetener, will elicit an insulin response. I recommend you keep the carbs as low as possible and eat a highly nutritious breakfast that contains plenty of protein and fat.

These simple rules will keep you happy and full of energy until lunch!

BAKED EGGS WITH BUTTER AND SAGE

You have never known the true flavor of sage until you fry it in butter. This simple herb transforms into a crispy blast of flavor. It's a perfect complement for the buttery flavor of baked eggs.

YIELD: 4 servings
PREPARATION TIME: 25 minutes

½ cup (115 g) unsalted butter

8 fresh sage leaves, washed and dried

4 eggs

½ tsp unrefined sea salt

Preheat the oven to 350°F (177°C).

In a medium skillet, melt the butter over medium heat, then place the sage leaves in the skillet and cook until they start to turn brown, being careful not to burn the sage or the butter. Reduce the heat until the leaves appear fully cooked, or about 3 minutes total.

Divide the sage leaves and melted butter among four small ramekins. Crack an egg into each ramekin, then sprinkle with salt. Bake until the whites are beginning to set and the yolks just start to get cloudy, about 15 minutes. Check the eggs frequently to make sure they do not overcook, as they will continue cooking in the warm ramekins when they come out of the oven.

Serve immediately with toasted Keto Lard Biscuits (page 135).

NOTE: If you are dairy intolerant, you can use ghee instead of butter in this recipe.

NUTRITIONAL VALUES:

Total Calories:	Total Carbs:	Fat:	Protein:	Fiber:	Net Carbs:
1134 kcal	9 g	109 g	29 g	8 g	1 g
Per portion 283.5	Per portion 2.3	Per portion 27.3	Per portion 7.3	Per portion 2	Per portion 0

EGGS AND ANCHOVIES

The humble anchovy; what a wonderful little fish! The anchovy is actually a secret superfood, rich in minerals, vitamins and essential fatty acids. In this recipe, the saltiness of the anchovy perfectly complements the mild flavor of the egg, and creates a real power breakfast.

YIELD: 2 portions
PREPARATION TIME: 5 minutes

2 tbsp (28 g) ghee or butter or coconut oil

4 large eggs

8 anchovy fillets, drained from oil

¼ tsp cayenne powder

In a large nonstick skillet, heat the cooking fat over high heat. Break the eggs into the skillet carefully, without breaking the yolks. Place 2 anchovy fillets around each egg yolk and cover the skillet with a tight-fitting lid. Lower the heat to medium and cook until the egg whites are set, and slightly browned at the edges, 1 to 2 minutes. Yolks should be still runny.

Serve with Keto Seed Bagels (page 139) or with Keto Naan Bread (page 136) and some avocado.

NUTRITIONAL VALUES:

Total Calories: 525 kcal	Total Carbs: 2 g	Fat: 42 g	Protein: 30 g	Fiber: 0 g	Net Carbs: 2 g
Per portion 262.5	Per portion 1	Per portion 21	Per portion 15	Per portion 0	Per portion 1

FRENCH SHAKSHUKA

Shakshuka is a Middle Eastern dish, made with fresh eggs, tomatoes, onions, garlic and peppers. The version I created is very similar, but instead of the classic ingredients, it uses Slow Cooker Ratatouille (page 116) as a base. Such a convenient way to use your veggie leftovers!

YIELD: 4 portions
PREPARATION TIME: 15 minutes

4 cups (842 g) Slow Cooker Ratatouille (page 116)

½ cup (118 ml) water

4 eggs

¼ tsp sweet paprika

¼ tsp unrefined sea salt

In a medium nonstick skillet, over medium heat, warm the ratatouille with the water, mixing well, until it starts to simmer, about 3 minutes.

Make four indents in the ratatouille with a spoon, so the eggs will stay in place and not run or break. Crack the eggs into the ratatouille, making sure the yolks stay intact, and sprinkle the egg yolks with the paprika and salt.

Cover the skillet with a tight-fitting lid and cook until the egg whites are set and the yolks reach desired consistency. For runny yolks, cook for about 8 minutes; for hard yolks, cook for about 10 minutes. Serve hot with toasted Keto Almond Butter Bread (page 132).

NUTRITIONAL VALUES:

Total Calories:	Total Carbs:	Fat:	Protein:	Fiber:	Net Carbs:
1018 kcal	53 g	62 g	37 g	19 g	34 g
Per portion	Per portion	Per portion	Per portion	Per portion	Per portion
254.5	13.2	15.5	9.2	4.7	8.5

CHOCOLATE GRANOLA

You would never know that this chocolaty, crunchy granola is grain-free and ketogenic!
The Keto lifestyle is not about depriving yourself; instead it is about enjoying flavors, foods,
life and your health! This recipe is a great source of fat for those days
when you are having a hard time reaching your fat goals.

YIELD: 10 servings
PREPARATION TIME: 25 minutes

1 cup (116 g) chopped walnuts

1 cup (170 g) chopped almonds

1 cup (116 g) chopped macadamias

1 cup (120 g) chopped pecans

1 cup (160 g) hemp seeds (see Note)

1 oz (28 g) baking chocolate, unsweetened

1 cup (218 g) coconut oil

¾ cup (98 g) confectioners-style Swerve sweetener

2 tbsp (14 g) unsweetened cocoa powder

Preheat the oven to 300°F (149°C).

Put the walnuts, almonds, macadamias, pecans, hemp seeds, chocolate, coconut oil, sweetener and cocoa powder in a large food processor and pulse a few times until well blended.

Spread the mix onto a cookie sheet, cover with parchment paper, and bake for 15 to 20 minutes, until golden brown. Turn off the oven, and for best results, leave there overnight.

The next day, take out the granola and remove from the cookie sheet with a wooden spatula. Store in an airtight container for up to 1 week.

NOTE: Hemp seeds are commonly found in health food stores, health food sections and online at Amazon or Thrive Market.

NUTRITIONAL VALUES:

Total Calories: 6561 kcal	Total Carbs: 119 g	Fat: 655 g	Protein: 132 g	Fiber: 78 g	Net Carbs: 41 g
Per portion 656	Per portion 11	Per portion 65	Per portion 13	Per portion 7.8	Per portion 4.1

KETO CEREAL

Sometimes you might still get the urge to have a sweet, comforting breakfast that reminds you of your childhood. This cereal recipe has a familiar cinnamon-crunch flavor, but it's made without sugar and contains a ton of very necessary fiber!

YIELD: 6 servings
PREPARATION TIME: 45 minutes

½ cup (38 g) finely grated coconut flakes

½ cup (68 g) ground flax seeds (see Notes)

½ cup (90 g) hemp hearts (see Notes)

½ cup (68 g) chia seeds

1 tbsp (8 g) ground cinnamon

3 tbsp (36 g) LAKANTO® or Swerve sweetener (see page 168)

1 cup (240 ml) water

3 tbsp (45 ml) melted butter

Preheat the oven to 300°F (149°C). Line a cookie sheet with parchment paper.

In a blender or food processor, combine the coconut flakes, flax seeds, hemp hearts, chia seeds, cinnamon and sweetener. Mix for about 5 seconds, then add the water, followed by the melted butter. Blend until all ingredients are combined and a smooth dough forms.

Spread the dough onto the cookie sheet using a rubber spatula, making it as even as possible until it's about ⅛ inch (3 mm) thick.

Bake for 15 minutes, then lower the heat and bake for 20 minutes longer. Turn off the oven and let the cereal cool inside, so it becomes extra crispy.

When the cereal has fully cooled, remove it from the cookie sheet, peel off the parchment paper carefully, then cut into ½-inch (13-mm) squares.

If it is still soft in the middle after cutting, place back on the tray, cook at 200°F (93°C) for another 10 minutes and let it cool in the oven.

Serve with unsweetened almond milk.

NOTES: For best results, you should grind your flax seeds just before you prepare the recipe. I use a coffee grinder for that.

Hemp hearts are commonly found in health food stores, health food sections and online at Amazon or Thrive Market.

NUTRITIONAL VALUES:

Total Calories:	Total Carbs:	Fat:	Protein:	Fiber:	Net Carbs:
1730 kcal	77 g	139 g	65 g	68 g	9 g
Per portion 288.3	Per portion 12.8	Per portion 23	Per portion 10.8	Per portion 11.3	Per portion 1.5

PORTOBELLO BENEDICTS

This is a fancy recipe great for weekends or for guests. You will experience the same great creamy flavor of conventional eggs benedict with barely any carbohydrates!

YIELD: 2 servings
PREPARATION TIME: 30 minutes

2 (3-inch [7-cm]-wide) Portobello mushroom caps

2 tsp (10 ml) olive oil

¾ tsp unrefined sea salt, divided

3 tbsp (45 ml) white vinegar

2 large pasture-raised eggs and 2 large pasture-raised egg yolks, extremely fresh

2 tbsp (30 ml) fresh lemon juice

4 tbsp (60 ml) melted organic butter

¼ tsp black pepper, freshly ground

2 large slices Prosciutto di Parma or Jamón Serrano

Preheat the broiler.

Brush the mushroom caps on both sides with olive oil and sprinkle with ½ teaspoon salt, then place face down on a broiler pan. Cook in the oven about 6 inches (15 cm) under the broiler until tender, turning once, about 7 minutes. Cover and put in a warm place until ready to use.

In a medium saucepan, bring at least 2 inches (5 cm) of water to a boil over high heat, then lower the heat to simmer. Add the white vinegar to the water. Using a spoon, swirl the water in the pan until a vortex forms. Gently break the egg onto a large metal spoon or into a ramekin and add it into the middle of the vortex. Keep stirring so the egg does not stick to the bottom, but keeps turning. Cook for 3 minutes, then remove with a slotted spoon, place on a plate and set aside. Repeat with the second egg.

Mix the egg yolks and lemon juice together with an electric or manual whisk in a stainless steel bowl until the mixture is starting to thicken and is almost double in volume, about 1 minute.

Place the bowl over a saucepan containing simmering water (or in a double boiler), over low heat. Continue to whisk rapidly, being careful not to let the eggs get too hot or they will scramble. Slowly pour in the melted butter and continue to whisk until the sauce is thickened. Add ¼ teaspoon of salt and fresh pepper and whisk until incorporated.

Assemble the benedicts on individual plates by placing the roasted mushroom on the bottom, folding a slice of prosciutto on top, then placing a poached egg on each. Complete with a generous tablespoon (15 ml) of the sauce.

Serve immediately.

NUTRITIONAL VALUES:

Total Calories:	Total Carbs:	Fat:	Protein:	Fiber:	Net Carbs:
858 kcal	15 g	78 g	29 g	3 g	12 g
Per portion	Per portion	Per portion	Per portion	Per portion	Per portion
429	7.5	39	14.5	1.5	6

SALMON BAGEL BENEDICTS

Salmon Bagel Benedicts make a scrumptious breakfast, perfect for a family Sunday brunch.
You will like it so much it might become your new favorite!

YIELD: 4 servings
PREPARATION TIME: 20 minutes

2 Keto Seed Bagels (page 139)

4 eggs and 2 large egg yolks, divided

1 tbsp (15 ml) fresh lemon juice

1 tbsp (15 ml) sauerkraut juice (can substitute with more lemon juice)

4 tbsp (60 ml) melted butter

¼ tsp unrefined sea salt

¼ tsp black pepper, freshly ground

1 tbsp (14 g) coconut oil

6 oz (170 g) smoked salmon or lox, divided in 4

Preheat the broiler.

Cut the bagels in half horizontally and place under the broiler to toast for about 2 minutes, or until the top is browned.

To make the hollandaise sauce, mix the two egg yolks, lemon juice and sauerkraut juice together with an electric or manual whisk in a stainless steel bowl until the mixture starts to thicken and almost doubles in volume, about a minute.

Place the bowl over a saucepan containing simmering water (or in a double boiler) over low heat. Continue to whisk rapidly, being careful not to let the eggs get too hot or they will scramble. Slowly pour in the melted butter and continue to whisk until the sauce is thickened. Add in the salt and fresh pepper and whisk until incorporated. Cover and put in a warm place until ready to use.

In a nonstick pan (preferably ceramic) over high heat, melt the coconut oil and add the four eggs. Fry until the whites are cooked and slightly brown at the edges but the yolks are still runny.

On a serving plate, place the toasted bagel halves, divide the salmon or lox on top of them, then place a fried egg on each half.

Drizzle some hollandaise sauce over each fried egg.

Serve immediately.

NUTRITIONAL VALUES:

Total Calories:	Total Carbs:	Fat:	Protein:	Fiber:	Net Carbs:
1975 kcal	46 g	154 g	105 g	27 g	19 g
Per portion	Per portion	Per portion	Per portion	Per portion	Per portion
493.7	11.5	38.5	26.2	6.7	4.7

SALMON KIMCHI SCRAMBLE

Kimchi is the ultimate superfood—it packs a nutritional punch! It provides tons of live friendly bacteria for your gut, as well as powerful antimicrobial and antiviral phytonutrients, enzymes and digestive aids. It's a miracle food when you add some quality protein and good fats to it; here is your real breakfast of champions!

YIELD: 4 servings
PREPARATION TIME: 15 minutes

1 tbsp (14 g) coconut oil

2½ oz (71 g) smoked salmon

1 cup (150 g) kimchi (homemade or no MSG)

4 eggs

¼ tsp salt

4 servings Easy Cauliflower Rice (page 103)

In a large nonstick skillet, heat the coconut oil over high heat. Crumble the salmon into small pieces and add to the skillet. Cook the salmon until slightly crunchy at the edges, about 3 minutes, then add the kimchi and sauté for another 3 or 4 minutes, until the kimchi is wilted.

Add the eggs and salt. At this point, you can either stir the eggs in loosely to scramble or leave the yolk intact if you prefer a runny yolk. Cook for about another minute until the whites are cooked.

Serve with the cauliflower rice on the side.

NOTE: If you prefer a big scramble, add the cauliflower rice to the skillet at the end and mix all together until hot. Serve immediately.

NUTRITIONAL VALUES:

Total Calories:	Total Carbs:	Fat:	Protein:	Fiber:	Net Carbs:
1000 kcal	36 g	75 g	54 g	13 g	23 g
Per portion	Per portion	Per portion	Per portion	Per portion	Per portion
250	9	18.7	13.5	3.2	5.7

BREAKFAST FRITTATA

Frittatas are a much-undervalued Italian classic. They can be breakfast, lunch . . . even dinner!
Once you get the frittata basics down, you can really get creative and use your veggie
and meat leftovers to improvise a last-minute meal.

YIELD: 8 servings   PREPARATION TIME: varies with ingredients

4 tbsp (60 ml) bacon drippings

¼ cup (33 g) sweet onion, sliced thin

8 large eggs

½ cup (118 ml) unsweetened almond milk, or another milk of choice

1 tsp unrefined sea salt

¼ tsp black pepper

4 Homemade Chicken Sausage patties (page 29), crumbled

8 oz (227 g) grilled zucchini, cut into small pieces, or another vegetable of choice

Preheat the oven to 350°F (177°C).

In a 10-inch (25-cm) cast-iron skillet, heat the bacon drippings over medium heat, then add the onion and cook until tender and transparent, about 5 minutes.

While the onion is cooking, whisk the eggs in a large bowl with the milk, salt and pepper. Whisk just enough to break the yolks and blend them with the whites, making sure you do not overmix. Add the meat and vegetables to the bowl and stir.

Add the egg mixture to the onions in the skillet, stirring for a few seconds to blend together. Cook over medium heat until the edges are cooked, about 5 minutes. Transfer the skillet to the oven and bake until the frittata is cooked in the middle, about 15 to 18 minutes. You can check it with a wooden toothpick to see if it's done. This can be eaten cold too.

NOTE: This recipe is great when meat and vegetable leftovers accumulate in the fridge and you want to reuse them.

Possible winning combinations include:
Asparagus + Thai meatballs + coconut oil + coconut milk
Diced avocado + shrimp + butter + almond milk

These different options will change the macros, however.

NUTRITIONAL VALUES:

Total Calories:	Total Carbs:	Fat:	Protein:	Fiber:	Net Carbs:
2224 kcal	30 g	188 g	94 g	3 g	27 g
Per portion	*Per portion*	*Per portion*	*Per portion*	*Per portion*	*Per portion*
278	3.7	23.5	11.7	0.3	3.3

SAVORY STUFFED BREAKFAST CRÊPES

This is a great recipe to reincarnate some meat leftovers in a totally unexpected way! Eating a substantial meal like this for breakfast will keep your blood sugar stable and your energy high until lunch.

YIELD: 10 servings (2 crêpes per serving)
PREPARATION TIME: 45 minutes

6 large eggs (plus more, if the batter becomes too thick)

1½ cups (355 ml) unsweetened almond milk

6 tbsp (90 ml) melted butter, ghee or coconut oil

¾ tsp salt, divided

2 tbsp (12 g) fine coconut flour

5 cups (1 kg) cooked leftover meat, roughly chopped

1 tsp butter

4 hardboiled eggs, roughly chopped

1 tbsp (2.5 g) fresh thyme, finely chopped

1 tbsp (2.5 g) fresh sage, finely chopped

½ tsp plus 1 tbsp (15 ml) cooking fat

Put the eggs, almond milk, butter, ¼ teaspoon salt and coconut flour in a blender and mix until well combined. Set the mixture aside and let rest for at least 20 minutes. The batter should have a runny consistency.

Place the leftover meat, butter, hard boiled eggs, thyme, sage and ½ teaspoon salt in a large food processor, and pulse until well blended but not overmixed. Set aside.

Heat a nonstick skillet over medium heat, and add ½ teaspoon of cooking fat to the skillet. When hot, add ¼ cup (60 ml) of the batter, then immediately swirl the pan to cover the bottom. Cook for about 1 minute, until golden on the bottom, then flip and cook for about 30 seconds on the other side. Stack the cooked crêpes on a plate covered with a pot's lid or parchment paper and a towel to keep warm and moist.

When all of the crêpes are cooked, proceed with filling. Add about ¼ cup (52 g) of the filling to the center of each crêpe in the shape of a cylinder. Take two sides of the crepe and fold them in over the filling, then roll the crêpe closed forming a tube.

Heat about 1 tablespoon (15 ml) of cooking fat in a large nonstick skillet and add the crêpes, about four at a time. Brown on all sides.

You can serve the crêpes with Creamy Tahini Sauce (page 145) or Creamy Avocado Dressing (page 144).

NUTRITIONAL VALUES

Total Calories:	Total Carbs:	Fat:	Protein:	Fiber:	Net Carbs:
3208 kcal	14 g	252 g	211 g	9 g	5 g
Per portion	Per portion	Per portion	Per portion	Per portion	Per portion
320.8	1.4	25.2	21	0.9	0.5

QUICK AND EASY LUNCHES

Thanks to our busy work lives, it's not uncommon for many people to eat lunch outside the house at least five days a week. Unfortunately, this is not always in the best interest of your health. Here you have a compilation of recipes that are both quick and easy to make. They are easily transportable and can even be served cold. Even if you are at home, you will be happy with the simplicity and speed of these meals. Plus, no nutrient is left behind!

CHICKEN SHAWARMA

I like to explore traditional flavors from many different countries. Trying new condiments keeps your diet varied and healthy, as we tend to develop sensitivities to the foods we eat over and over. I hope you will love this Mediterranean combination of spices!

YIELD: 4 servings
PREPARATION TIME: 20 minutes

½ tsp ground cumin

½ tsp ground coriander

½ tsp cayenne

¼ tsp ground cinnamon

½ tsp freshly ground black pepper

1 tsp unrefined sea salt

2 tbsp (30 ml) olive oil

1½ lb (681 g) boneless chicken thighs, cut into 1-inch (2.5-cm) strips

Preheat the oven to 425°F (218°C).

In a large bowl, combine the cumin, coriander, cayenne, cinnamon, pepper, salt and olive oil and mix well. Add the chicken, toss and coat well.

Spread the chicken on a cookie sheet. Bake until the chicken is done but still juicy, about 15 minutes.

Serve the chicken on Keto Naan Bread (page 136) drizzled with a couple of tablespoons (30 ml) of Creamy Tahini Sauce (page 145).

NUTRITIONAL VALUES:

Total Calories: 1175 kcal	Total Carbs: 4 g	Fat: 96 g	Protein: 83 g	Fiber: 2 g	Net Carbs: 2 g
Per portion 293.7	Per portion 1	Per portion 24	Per portion 20.7	Per portion 0.5	Per portion 0.5

CHICKEN SAUSAGE WRAPS WITH KETO PALEO MAYO

Use your already-made sausage for this super quick and tasty lunch idea!
If you did not shape your sausage into cylinders, cut the patties in half for easier wrapping.
This can be premade to bring to work.

YIELD: 4 servings
PREPARATION TIME: 10 minutes

1 tbsp (14 g) butter or ghee

4 Homemade Chicken Sausage patties (page 29)

4 large romaine lettuce leaves, washed and dried

2 tbsp (30 ml) Keto Paleo Mayo (page 151)

In a nonstick skillet, melt the butter over high heat. Cook the patties until browned on top and done all the way through, turning once, about 5 minutes.

Arrange the romaine leaves on individual plates, spread them with the Keto Paleo Mayo, and then arrange the sausage in the middle of the leaves.

Wrap leaves around the sausage and serve immediately or refrigerate and eat the same day.

NUTRITIONAL VALUES:

Total Calories:	Total Carbs:	Fat:	Protein:	Fiber:	Net Carbs:
1692 kcal	8 g	119 g	46 g	2 g	6 g
Per portion 423	Per portion 2	Per portion 29.7	Per portion 11.5	Per portion 0.5	Per portion 1.5

CURRIED EGG SALAD ROLLS

I learned to put curry powder on eggs when I lived in Germany. Adding curry powder to boiled eggs creates a whole new flavor combination—it is simple but exotic and savory, yet creamy and satisfying. This easy lunch contains a lot of healthy fats, perfect for your Keto lifestyle. Remember that the latest research proves that dietary cholesterol is not only beneficial; it's necessary for a healthy body and brain.

YIELD: 4 servings
PREPARATION TIME: 5 minutes

4 eggs, hard boiled

2 tsp (5 g) curry powder

2 tbsp (30 ml) Keto Paleo Mayo (page 151)

⅛ tsp unrefined sea salt

⅛ tsp black pepper

4 slices roasted turkey breast

In a small food processor, pulse the eggs, curry powder, Keto Paleo Mayo, salt and pepper until coarsely chopped but blended together.

Spread one quarter of the egg salad on each turkey slice and roll up. Secure with a toothpick. Serve immediately.

NUTRITIONAL VALUES:

Total Calories:	Total Carbs:	Fat:	Protein:	Fiber:	Net Carbs:
811 kcal	3 g	57 g	71 g	2 g	1 g
Per portion	Per portion	Per portion	Per portion	Per portion	Per portion
202.7	0.7	14.2	17.7	0	0

EASY STEAK ROLL UPS WITH KETO PALEO MAYO

I love steak for lunch, since it keeps me from getting hungry until dinner, avoiding those nasty midday energy crashes. While you might get bored with plain ol' steak, these roll ups will entertain your palate with a crunchy pickle and delicious, creamy mayo!

YIELD: 6 roll ups (1 roll up=1 serving)
PREPARATION TIME: 20 minutes

1 lb (454 g) skirt steak, 1 inch (2.5 cm) thick, at room temperature

2 tbsp (10 g) unrefined coarse sea salt

6 lactofermented mini dill pickles (see Note)

6 cherry tomatoes

6 tbsp (90 ml) Keto Paleo Mayo (page 151)

Place the meat on a plate and sprinkle with salt on both sides. Do not rub the salt in or it will be too salty.

Heat a cast-iron grill pan over high heat until very hot. Sear the steak on the grill pan for about 3 minutes per side, until medium rare.

Remove the steak from the grill pan, shaking off the excess salt, and place on a warm plate. Cover and let rest for about 10 minutes.

Slice the steak in two across the thickness, in order to create two large thin slices, then cut the thinner slices into three long strips each.

Slice the pickles in half lengthwise, and slice the tomatoes into four.

Spread a tablespoon (15 ml) of Keto Paleo Mayo on each strip of steak, then place a pickle half and two or three pieces of tomato on it. Roll up and secure with a toothpick.

NOTE: Lactofermented dill pickles can be found in most health food stores, in the refrigerated section.

NUTRITIONAL VALUES:

Total Calories:	Total Carbs:	Fat:	Protein:	Fiber:	Net Carbs:
2212 kcal	5 g	188 g	125 g	2 g	3 g
Per portion 368.6	Per portion 0.8	Per portion 31.3	Per portion 20.8	Per portion 0.3	Per portion 0.5

TURKEY AND AVOCADO ROLL UPS

This is a great recipe for a last-minute lunch or even a great savory breakfast. You can make the roasted turkey breast ahead and then just slice from it for several meals! You can add fresh herbs like parsley or cilantro to the rolls to add flavor and some valuable phytonutrients.

YIELD: 4 servings
PREPARATION TIME: 5 minutes

4 oz (112 g) roasted turkey breast, in 4 slices

4 tbsp (60 ml) Keto Paleo Mayo (page 151)

1 large avocado

Pinch of unrefined sea salt or Himalayan salt

Pinch of black pepper, finely ground

Lay out the turkey slices on a plate large enough to accommodate them. Spread the Keto Paleo Mayo in a thick layer over each slice. Slice the avocado and place on top of the mayo. Sprinkle with salt and pepper.

Carefully roll up the slices into four rolls. Cut each roll into about four pieces and enjoy immediately.

NOTE: If you like a little spice, you can add a sprinkle of cayenne pepper on the turkey slices.

NUTRITIONAL VALUES:

Total Calories:	Total Carbs:	Fat:	Protein:	Fiber:	Net Carbs:
1083 kcal	12 g	94 g	53 g	10 g	2 g
Per portion 270.7	Per portion 3	Per portion 23.5	Per portion 13.3	Per portion 2.5	Per portion 0.5

MIDDLE EASTERN STEAK ROLL UPS WITH TAHINI SAUCE

I think there are never too many ideas for tasty, nutritious lunches that can be made quickly or made ahead. If your days are as busy as mine, you will appreciate this recipe. Eggplant makes these roll ups especially tasty and filling. Combined with lots of protein and healthy fats, this lunch will keep you happy until dinnertime, no matter how busy you get.

YIELD: 6 roll ups (1 roll up=1 serving)
PREPARATION TIME: 20 minutes

1 lb (454 g) skirt steak, 1 inch (2.5 cm) thick, at room temperature

2 tbsp (10 g) unrefined coarse sea salt

12 slices fresh eggplant, about ½ inch (1 cm) thick

¼ cup (60 ml) extra virgin olive oil

TAHINI SAUCE

¼ cup (63 g) tahini

1 lemon, juiced

1 clove garlic, pressed

¼ tsp unrefined sea salt

¼ tsp freshly ground black pepper

Pinch of cayenne pepper

Place the meat on a plate and sprinkle with salt on both sides. Do not rub the salt in or it will be too salty.

Heat a cast-iron grill pan over high heat until very hot. Sear the steak on the grill pan for about 3 minutes per side, until medium rare.

Remove the steak from the grill pan, shaking off the excess salt, and place on a warm plate. Cover and let rest for about 10 minutes.

While the steak is resting, brush the slices of eggplant with the olive oil on both sides, then grill in the same grill pan until they are tender and cooked, about 2 minutes per side.

Set aside to cool.

Slice the steak across to create two large thinner slices, then cut the thinner slices into two to three long pieces each.

To prepare the tahini sauce, add the tahini, lemon juice, garlic, sea salt, black pepper and cayenne pepper to a bowl and mix with a fork until creamy and well blended.

Place two slices of eggplant on each strip of steak, then place a tablespoon (15 ml) of sauce on the eggplant. Roll up and secure with a toothpick.

These can be served immediately or eaten cold.

NUTRITIONAL VALUES:

Total Calories:	Total Carbs:	Fat:	Protein:	Fiber:	Net Carbs:
3763 kcal	46 g	351 g	130 g	22 g	24 g
Per portion 627	Per portion 7.6	Per portion 58.5	Per portion 21.6	Per portion 3.6	Per portion 4

SEARED CARPACCIO SALAD

In Italy, "carpaccio" means a dish with thinly sliced raw beef or fish. Because some people might have a hard time eating raw meat, I modified this recipe a bit, so you can still get the benefits of raw protein with a burst of steak flavor!

YIELD: 2 portions
PREPARATION TIME: 15 minutes

6 oz (170 g) filet mignon

½ tsp unrefined sea salt, plus more for sprinkling

¼ tsp black pepper, plus more for sprinkling

1 tbsp (14 g) butter, softened, divided

4 cups (80 g) baby arugula

3 tbsp (45 ml) olive oil

2 tbsp (30 ml) balsamic vinegar

¼ cup (35 g) crushed macadamias

Bring the filet to room temperature, about 30 minutes. Sprinkle the filet with salt and pepper.

Heat a cast-iron grill pan over high heat until a drop of water sizzles on it. Place the filet in the pan and cook for 3 to 4 minutes, then turn. Put half of the butter on the top of the filet and cook for another 3 to 4 minutes. Remove from the grill and place on a warm plate. Put the rest of the butter on the filet and cover. Allow the filet to rest for about 5 minutes.

While the steak is resting, put the baby arugula in a bowl and toss with the oil, vinegar, salt and pepper. Divide the arugula into two bowls.

Slice the filet against the grain into very thin slices with a sharp knife. Lay half on each plate on top of the salad, then sprinkle with the macadamias.

NOTE: The filet in the recipe should be rare to medium rare. You can vary cooking time to modify desired doneness, but I do recommend keeping it as rare as possible, to take advantage of the health benefits of eating raw protein.

NUTRITIONAL VALUES:

Total Calories:	Total Carbs:	Fat:	Protein:	Fiber:	Net Carbs:
1181 kcal	17 g	109 g	41 g	5 g	12 g
Per portion	Per portion	Per portion	Per portion	Per portion	Per portion
590.5	8.5	54.5	20.5	2.5	6

SHRIMP AND ROMAINE SAUTÉ

When I am really short on time, but feel bored with the usual fare, I turn to recipes like this one. This dish has savory-sweet, Chinese-inspired flavors, but none of the unhealthy ingredients you might find in a Chinese restaurant. Make sure you have all the ingredients handy, and this meal will be ready in a flash.

YIELD: 4 servings
PREPARATION TIME: 10 minutes

3 tbsp (42 g) coconut oil

4 cloves garlic, pressed

1 tbsp (15 g) fresh ginger, peeled and very finely chopped

1 lb (454 g) raw, large shrimp, shelled

2 small heads clean romaine lettuce, cut in 4 lengthwise

¼ cup (35 g) crushed macadamia nuts

¼ cup (60 ml) chicken broth

2 tbsp (30 ml) coconut aminos (see Note)

1 tbsp (15 ml) rice vinegar

1 tbsp (12 g) Swerve or LAKANTO® (see page 168)

1 tsp red pepper flakes

Heat the coconut oil in a 12-inch (30-cm) nonstick skillet over high heat. Add the garlic and ginger to the pan and sauté for about a minute, stirring often. Add the shrimp to the pan and cook, stirring until almost cooked, about 2 minutes. Add the romaine lettuce to the pan and cook until wilted, about 2 minutes. Add the macadamia nuts, chicken broth, coconut aminos, rice vinegar, sweetener and red pepper flakes to the pan and cook, stirring constantly, for another 2 minutes.

Serve immediately. This recipe pairs nicely with Easy Cauliflower Rice (page 103).

NOTE: Coconut aminos are a great soy-free substitution for soy sauce. Find them in most health food stores or on the Internet.

NUTRITIONAL VALUES:

Total Calories: 1441 kcal	Total Carbs: 60 g	Fat: 100 g	Protein: 84 g	Fiber: 26 g	Net Carbs: 34 g
Per portion 360	Per portion 15	Per portion 25	Per portion 21	Per portion 6.5	Per portion 8.5

SHRIMP CAESAR SALAD

Caesar salad is my favorite salad, and I could probably eat it every day. I love it with chicken, salmon and grilled shrimp. This version is a little different, as it doesn't call for croutons, but you can always use pork rinds as a substitute if you are missing the crunch.

YIELD: 4 servings
PREPARATION TIME: 20 minutes

1 egg yolk at room temperature

1 tbsp (15 ml) fresh lemon juice

1 tsp Dijon mustard

2 cloves garlic, pressed

4 anchovy fillets, cut into small pieces

8 tbsp (120 ml) avocado oil

8 tbsp (112 g) butter

1 tbsp (7 g) lemon zest

16 large raw shrimp, cleaned, peeled

½ tsp unrefined sea salt

¼ tsp black pepper

6 cups (300 g) romaine hearts, cut into 1-inch (2.5-cm) pieces

In the cup of an immersion blender, place the egg yolk, lemon juice, mustard, garlic and anchovies. Insert the blender stick and stand it on the egg yolk, then pour the avocado oil carefully on top. Start the blender on low, without moving it from its position. The egg yolk should slowly emulsify with the oil, creating a mayonnaise. Set aside.

In a 10-inch (25-cm) saucepan, melt the butter over low heat, then add the lemon zest and carefully place the shrimp in the butter. Sprinkle with salt and pepper. Cook only until the shrimp turns pink, about 30 seconds, then turn and cook for another 30 seconds. Cooking the shrimp longer will make it tough and rubbery.

Divide the romaine lettuce into four bowls, place the shrimp onto the lettuce and drizzle with the dressing, dividing it equally amongst the bowls.

Serve immediately.

NOTE: If the dressing does not emulsify into a mayonnaise, you can start over by placing a tablespoon (15 ml) of Keto Paleo Mayo (page 151) in a clean container (a small mason jar with a wide mouth is perfect for the job), then slowly add the dressing on top while running the immersion blender. It should easily emulsify.

NUTRITIONAL VALUES:

Total Calories:	Total Carbs:	Fat:	Protein:	Fiber:	Net Carbs:
2041 kcal	13 g	213 g	31 g	6 g	7 g
Per portion	Per portion	Per portion	Per portion	Per portion	Per portion
510.2	3.2	53.2	7.7	1.5	1.75

STRACCETTI CON LA RUCHETTA (SLICED STEAK WITH ARUGULA)

Straccetti con la ruchetta is another recipe from my home country of Italy. This is one of the quickest lunches you can ever prepare, but do not be deceived by the simplicity. The arugula gives it a very distinct flavor, which is not diminished by cooking. Arugula is also packed with nutrition: It contains high levels of folic acid and antioxidants like Vitamins C, K and A, plus potassium, manganese, iron and calcium. No wonder we love it!

YIELD: 4 servings
PREPARATION TIME: 15 minutes

1 lb (454 g) boneless sirloin steak, about 1 inch (2.5 cm) thick, at room temperature

3 tbsp (45 ml) extra virgin olive oil

2 cloves garlic, peeled and smashed

1 sprig fresh rosemary

3 oz (84 g) baby arugula

¼ tsp unrefined sea salt

¼ tsp freshly ground black pepper

Cut the steak against the grain of the meat, into ½-inch (1-cm)-thick slices, and set aside.

Heat the olive oil with the garlic and rosemary in a heavy 12-inch (30-cm) skillet over medium heat. Stir the garlic often until it is golden brown, about 4 minutes.

Raise the heat to high and add the meat to the skillet. Sauté, stirring often, to brown evenly, about 3 minutes.

Add the arugula to the skillet, season with salt and pepper and sauté until barely wilted, for about another minute.

Serve immediately.

NUTRITIONAL VALUES:

Total Calories:	Total Carbs:	Fat:	Protein:	Fiber:	Net Carbs:
1269 kcal	5 g	98 g	90 g	1 g	4 g
Per portion 317.2	Per portion 1.2	Per portion 24.5	Per portion 22.5	Per portion 0	Per portion 1

WARM SEAFOOD SALAD

This delicious Warm Seafood Salad takes inspiration from the cuisine of the French Riviera, very near the part of Italy where I spent my childhood. I love the combination of tomatoes and black olives with arugula, all bold distinct flavors that remind us of the Mediterranean. The combination of butter and olive oil is also distinctly French–Italian, and it has the practical purpose of not burning the butter while you cook.

YIELD: 4 portions
PREPARATION TIME: 15 minutes

1 tbsp (14 g) butter

1 tbsp (15 ml) olive oil

1 tbsp (2.5 g) fresh thyme leaves, finely chopped

1 cup (160 g) cherry tomatoes, halved

½ cup (70 g) Kalamata olives, pitted and halved

1 lb (454 g) frozen seafood mix, defrosted (shrimp, scallop, squid)

¼ tsp unrefined sea salt

4 cups (80 g) baby arugula

In a large nonstick skillet, melt the butter over high heat with the olive oil and thyme. When the butter starts to foam, add the tomatoes and sauté until they begin to wilt, about 2 minutes.

Add the olives, seafood mix and salt to the pan, cover with a tight-fitting lid and cook until the seafood is done but still tender, about 5 minutes. Make sure you do not overcook or it will be tough and rubbery. The seafood should still have a lot of cooking juices, and that is okay, as you will use them instead of a dressing.

Divide the arugula into four serving bowls and pour some of the seafood mix on each. Serve immediately.

NOTE: You can use a baby greens mix instead of arugula, or use your favorite lettuce. Romaine is a great fit for this recipe.

NUTRITIONAL VALUES:

Total Calories: 820 kcal	Total Carbs: 18 g	Fat: 57 g	Protein: 68 g	Fiber: 6 g	Net Carbs: 12 g
Per portion 205	*Per portion* 4.5	*Per portion* 14.5	*Per portion* 17	*Per portion* 1.5	*Per portion* 3

SIDE DISHES, SOUPS AND SNACKS

My readers are always hungry for healthy low-carb veggie recipes. It can be difficult navigating the abundance of vegetables available while keeping your carb count low. With these recipes I kept the focus on the low-carb/high-fiber vegetables. Fiber is important to help your gut stay healthy through the process of Keto adaptation. Side dishes will also make your diet more varied and interesting.

I also have a special place in my heart for soups.
They feed the soul as well as the body.

ARUGULA STRACCIATELLA SOUP

Believe it or not, this soup makes an excellent breakfast! During the cold winter months, there is nothing better than starting your day with a hearty, savory soup. It provides some good protein, hydration, electrolytes and phytonutrients. And, it will warm you to the core!

YIELD: 4 servings
PREPARATION TIME: 10 minutes

4 cups (1 L) store-bought or homemade chicken stock

2 eggs

2 oz (56 g) baby arugula

Pinch of black pepper

Unrefined sea salt as needed

4 tbsp (60 ml) olive oil

Heat the stock in a medium saucepan over high heat until it reaches a rolling boil.

While heating the stock, whisk the eggs until foamy. When the stock is boiling, add the eggs in a stream, stirring continuously. Stir for another minute until the egg is cooked, then add the arugula and turn off the heat. Add the black pepper and salt. Keep stirring until the arugula is wilted, about 30 seconds.

Sprinkle the olive oil on the plated soup right before serving. Serve very hot.

NUTRITIONAL VALUES:

Total Calories:	Total Carbs:	Fat:	Protein:	Fiber:	Net Carbs:
916 kcal	33 g	73 g	46 g	7 g	2 g
Per portion	Per portion	Per portion	Per portion	Per portion	Per portion
229	8.3	18.3	11.5	1.8	0.5

BAKED FENNEL

Side dishes do not have to be complicated to be tasty. Another recipe from Italy, this one is from my beloved grandmother. As you might have noticed, I love "Keto-fying" my childhood recipes and bringing you a taste of the original Italian flavors I grew up with and the wholesomeness of traditional home-cooked foods.

YIELD: 4 servings
PREPARATION TIME: 50 minutes

1 whole fennel bulb

1 tbsp (15 ml) olive oil

1 tbsp (15 ml) melted coconut oil

¼ tsp unrefined sea salt

Preheat the oven to 350°F (177°C). Wash the fennel and trim off the green tops and hard base.

Slice the fennel lengthwise in ⅓-inch (8-mm)-thick slices. Lay the fennel slices on a nonstick cookie sheet and pour the oils on top, coating evenly on top and bottom, flipping them once. Sprinkle salt on top.

Bake until caramelized and brown, about 45 minutes, flipping once.

NOTE: I like my fennel nice and brown so all the sugars caramelize, but you might prefer it less done, so you can adjust cooking time depending on desired doneness.

NUTRITIONAL VALUES:

Total Calories:	Total Carbs:	Fat:	Protein:	Fiber:	Net Carbs:
322 kcal	17 g	28 g	3 g	7 g	21 g
Per portion 80.5	Per portion 4.3	Per portion 7	Per portion 0.8	Per portion 1.8	Per portion 5.3

BROWN-BUTTER SALAD

You might not love green salads, until you try this one! Butter lettuce could
not have a more appropriate name, as the leaves literally melt in your mouth. Add nutty
brown butter on top and you will get something close to salad heaven. The good
fat and low carb content make it a great Keto dish!

YIELD: 4 servings
PREPARATION TIME: 15 minutes

4 cups (161 g) butter lettuce (or
another mild green lettuce)

¼ cup (57 g) butter

1 tbsp (15 ml) white wine vinegar

1 tbsp (4 g) chives, finely chopped

Wash the lettuce in lukewarm water to help bring the leaves to room
temperature. Drain and spin in a salad spinner.

Put the butter in a small saucepan and melt over very low heat. Keep
cooking until it starts to brown, about 2 more minutes.

When the butter begins to brown, pour the vinegar into the saucepan,
whisking with a wire whisk, scraping the brown bits from the bottom.
Add the chives to the pan, stir and remove from heat.

Put the dried lettuce in a salad bowl and drizzle with the brown-butter
dressing. Serve immediately.

NUTRITIONAL VALUES:

Total Calories:	Total Carbs:	Fat:	Protein:	Fiber:	Net Carbs:
604 kcal	1 g	44 g	8 g	8 g	0 g
Per portion	Per portion	Per portion	Per portion	Per portion	Per portion
151	0	11	2	2	0

EASY CAULIFLOWER RICE

This is the quickest, tastiest way to prepare cauliflower rice, an almost indispensable side dish for curries and stews! Cauliflower rice is a great low-carb alternative to rice; it also provides a good amount of fiber and it's rich in choline (a B vitamin), minerals and other vitamins.

YIELD: 4 servings
PREPARATION TIME: 15 minutes

1 large head cauliflower

4 tbsp (60 ml) olive oil or coconut oil, plus more for cooking

½ tsp unrefined sea salt

Clean the cauliflower and remove the leaves and hard stems, leaving only the florets and softer stems. Cut into large pieces and place in a food processor. Pulse a few times, until it resembles the texture of rice. Make sure you do not overprocess and turn the cauliflower into a puree.

Heat the olive or coconut oil in a large nonstick ceramic skillet over high heat. When the oil is hot add the riced cauliflower and sauté until cooked, about 10 minutes. Sprinkle with the sea salt. If you like the rice slightly browned, sauté for an additional 5 minutes.

NOTE: In this recipe, you can use olive oil or coconut oil, depending on which dish you are planning to serve the cauliflower rice with. Use coconut oil to pair with a curry, and use olive oil for Mediterranean flavors and dishes. You can get creative and sauté your cauliflower in bacon fat, schmaltz (poultry fat) or ghee for a variety of flavor outcomes.

NUTRITIONAL VALUES:

Total Calories:	Total Carbs:	Fat:	Protein:	Fiber:	Net Carbs:
710 kcal	45 g	57 g	17 g	21 g	24 g
Per portion	Per portion	Per portion	Per portion	Per portion	Per portion
177.5	11.2	14.2	4.2	5.3	6

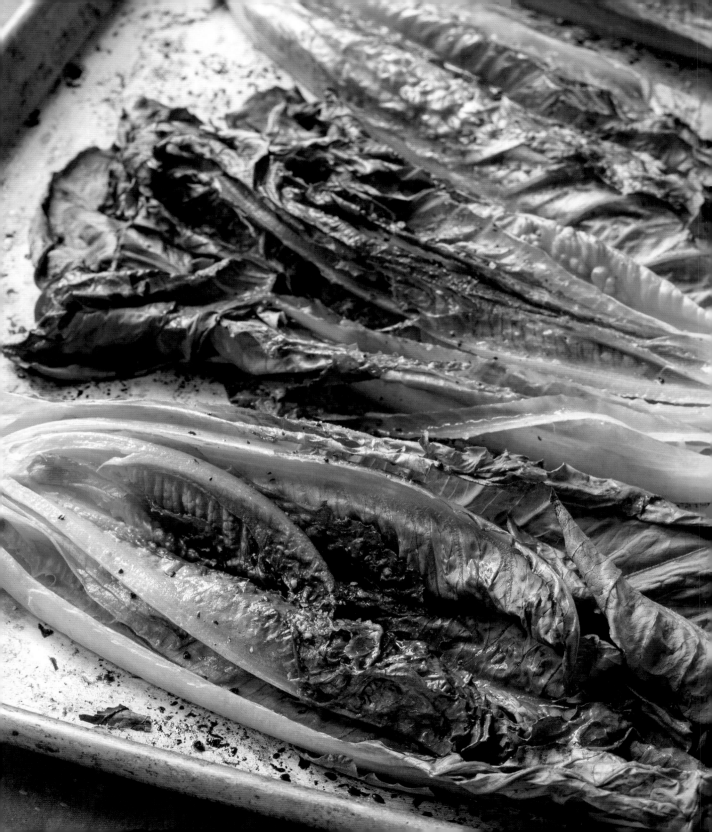

CAESAR ROASTED ROMAINE

Cooked romaine lettuce is one of the best-kept secrets of the culinary world! It turns out this lettuce is just as delicious raw as it is cooked, and the cooking can be done in a number of ways, from baked to stir-fried. Here is a quick and very flavorful way to do it.

YIELD: 4 servings
PREPARATION TIME: 20 minutes

4 tbsp (60 ml) olive oil, plus more for oiling cookie sheet

2 heads romaine lettuce

2 inches (5 cm) anchovy paste or 2 anchovy fillets, pressed through a garlic press

2 cloves garlic, pressed

Freshly ground black pepper, to taste

Preheat the oven to 400°F (204°C). Oil a cookie sheet.

Wash the romaine lettuce, then slice the heads in half lengthwise. Lay on the cookie sheet, cut side up.

In a small bowl, mix the anchovy paste, garlic and olive oil, and whisk with a fork until smoothly blended. With a pastry brush or a fork, brush the anchovy mix on the lettuce, dividing it evenly. Sprinkle with black pepper on top.

Bake until wilted and brown at the edges, about 10 to 15 minutes, depending on lettuce size.

Serve as a side to any meat or fish main course. Great with simple proteins like the Homemade Chicken Sausage patties (page 29).

NUTRITIONAL VALUES:

Total Calories:	Total Carbs:	Fat:	Protein:	Fiber:	Net Carbs:
708 kcal	44 g	56 g	17 g	26 g	18 g
Per portion	Per portion	Per portion	Per portion	Per portion	Per portion
177	11	14	4.2	6.5	4.5

CREAMY ROASTED ASPARAGUS SOUP

This soup boasts a velvety texture and a bold but smooth garlic flavor. It will warm your bones and fill your belly like a real meal. Plenty of good fat and protein provide a good balance for the slightly higher carb content, so your energy remains stable. You can eat it for dinner as it is the most appropriate time of the day for a higher carb dish!

YIELD: 6 servings
PREPARATION TIME: 25 minutes

2 lb (908 g) young asparagus, bottoms trimmed

5 cloves garlic, peeled

2 tbsp (30 ml) olive oil

½ tsp unrefined sea salt

¼ tsp black pepper

3 cups (720 ml) chicken broth

1 cup (240 ml) unsweetened almond milk

1 tbsp (14 g) butter or ghee

Preheat the oven to 450°F (232°C).

On a baking sheet, toss the asparagus and garlic with the olive oil, salt and pepper. Roast until the asparagus is tender, about 10 minutes.

Remove from the oven and put the asparagus and garlic in a blender with the chicken broth, almond milk and butter or ghee. Blend, and when smooth and velvety, transfer the asparagus to a soup pot. Cook over medium heat until it reaches a boil, about 7 minutes. Adjust for flavor with more salt and pepper.

Serve with Herbed Croutons (page 131).

NOTE: If your blender is not big enough, use an immersion blender or puree the soup in several batches.

NUTRITIONAL VALUES:

Total Calories:	Total Carbs:	Fat:	Protein:	Fiber:	Net Carbs:
540 kcal	42 g	21 g	37 g	21 g	21 g
Per portion	Per portion	Per portion	Per portion	Per portion	Per portion
90	7	3.5	6.1	3.5	3.5

DANDELION SALAD WITH BALSAMIC PANCETTA DRESSING

I love all the medicinal proprieties of dandelion! It's a diuretic and a great liver cleanser. The bitter taste might take a moment to get used to, but I find that the smooth flavor of the pancetta makes a perfect complement.

YIELD: 4 servings
PREPARATION TIME: 20 minutes

8 cups (322 g) fresh dandelion leaves, washed and roughly chopped

6 oz (170 g) sliced pancetta

2 oz (56 g) shallot, sliced thin

2 tbsp (30 ml) balsamic vinegar

½ tsp unrefined sea salt

¼ tsp freshly ground black pepper

Place the dandelion leaves in a large salad bowl.

Cut the pancetta into ½-inch (1-cm) strips. Place them in a nonstick skillet over low heat and cook until all the fat renders and the pancetta turns brown and crisp, about 5 minutes. Remove the pancetta bits from the skillet, leaving the fat behind, and place them on top of the dandelion greens.

Add the shallots to the skillet with the fat and cook over low heat until they are transparent and fully cooked, about 5 minutes. Add the balsamic vinegar, salt and pepper to the skillet and cook for 1 to 2 minutes. Pour the hot balsamic dressing over the dandelion greens and pancetta and serve immediately.

NUTRITIONAL VALUES:

Total Calories:	Total Carbs:	Fat:	Protein:	Fiber:	Net Carbs:
883 kcal	57 g	75 g	24 g	17 g	40 g
Per portion	Per portion	Per portion	Per portion	Per portion	Per portion
220.7	14.2	18.7	6	4.3	10

ENDIVES WITH PERSILLADE

Similar to a gremolata, this persillade makes a wonderful topping. You will love its bright, tangy flavor, and the phytonutrients, minerals and fiber it provides. You can use it to top salads and other cooked vegetables. It is great served on fish as well.

YIELD: 8 servings
PREPARATION TIME: 20 minutes

8 endives

4 tbsp (56 g) butter

¼ tsp nutmeg

1 tsp coriander

1½ cups (90 g) fresh parsley, finely chopped

4 tbsp (21 g) coarsely chopped almonds

1 tbsp (15 ml) Dijon mustard

1 lemon, zested

1 tbsp (15 ml) lemon juice

4 tbsp (60 ml) olive oil

½ tsp unrefined sea salt

¼ tsp black pepper

Preheat the broiler.

Wash and trim the hard base off of the endives. In a large skillet, melt the butter with the nutmeg and coriander over medium heat, then sauté the endives for about 1 minute. Add enough hot water to cover the bottom of the pan, then cover with a lid and simmer over low heat for about 8 minutes.

While the endives are cooking, combine the parsley, almonds, mustard, lemon zest, juice and olive oil in a bowl, and blend well. Season with salt and pepper.

Remove the endives from the cooking juices and place in an oven-safe dish. Cover with the persillade, then place under the broiler for about 3 minutes, making sure the topping does not burn. Serve hot.

NUTRITIONAL VALUES:

Total Calories:	Total Carbs:	Fat:	Protein:	Fiber:	Net Carbs:
2215 kcal	168 g	156 g	74 g	144 g	24 g
Per portion 276.8	Per portion 21	Per portion 19.5	Per portion 9.3	Per portion 18	Per portion 3

HERBED CAULIFLOWER RICE

Herbed Cauliflower Rice is a flavorful spin on the classic cauliflower rice. It makes a great side for chicken and fish dishes, or for any main dish with softer flavors. In addition to all the benefits of normal cauliflower rice, this recipe provides extra potassium from the cilantro, which is much needed especially when your body is adapting to a ketogenic diet.

YIELD: 4 servings
PREPARATION TIME: 15 minutes

1 large head cauliflower

4 tbsp (60 ml) olive oil or coconut oil

1 clove garlic, finely chopped

½ cup (8 g) fresh cilantro, finely chopped

½ tsp unrefined sea salt

Clean the cauliflower and remove the leaves and hard stems, leaving only the florets and softer stems. Cut into large pieces and place in a food processor. Pulse a few times, until it resembles the texture of rice. Make sure you do not overprocess and turn the cauliflower into a puree.

Heat the olive or coconut oil in a large nonstick ceramic skillet over high heat. When the oil is hot, add the garlic and sauté until fragrant, about 1 minute. Add the riced cauliflower, cilantro and salt, and sauté until cooked, about 10 minutes, stirring often so it does not stick to the bottom or burn.

NUTRITIONAL VALUES:

Total Calories:	Total Carbs:	Fat:	Protein:	Fiber:	Net Carbs:
725 kcal	52 g	58 g	20 g	25 g	27 g
Per portion 181.2	Per portion 13	Per portion 14.5	Per portion 5	Per portion 6.2	Per portion 6.7

RADISHES WITH CUMIN BUTTER SAUCE

Instead of using carb-loaded potatoes, radishes can provide a wonderful comforting side dish! Try these braised radishes delicately infused with nutty and tangy cumin and you may have a new favorite side dish.

YIELD: 4 servings
PREPARATION TIME: 20 minutes

20 medium radishes, plus optional greens

1 tbsp (4 g) whole cumin seeds or 2 tsp (5 g) cumin powder

1 cup (240 ml) homemade chicken or beef broth

¼ tsp unrefined sea salt

¼ tsp black pepper

¼ cup (60 ml) olive oil

2 tbsp (28 g) butter

1 tsp lemon zest

Wash the radishes and trim their ends.

In a medium saucepan, toast the cumin seeds over medium heat until fragrant, about 30 seconds. Add the radishes, broth, salt and pepper to the pan, and bring to a gentle simmer. Simmer over low heat with a closed lid until the radishes are tender, about 8 to 10 minutes. Remove the radishes from the pot, and set aside the cooking liquid. Cut the radishes in quarters

In a medium skillet, heat the olive oil over high heat. When hot, sauté the radishes until lightly browned on all sides, about 2 minutes per side.

Put the saucepan with the cooking liquid back on the stove and cook over high heat until the liquid reduces by half, about 3 minutes. Add the radish greens, if desired.

Whisk in the butter with a wire whisk, then add the lemon zest. Serve the radishes warm, drizzled with the reduced butter sauce.

NUTRITIONAL VALUES:

Total Calories:	Total Carbs:	Fat:	Protein:	Fiber:	Net Carbs:
792 kcal	8 g	87 g	11 g	3 g	5 g
Per portion	Per portion	Per portion	Per portion	Per portion	Per portion
198	2	21.7	2.7	0.8	1.2

SALT AND PEPPER ASPARAGUS

This is one of my all-time favorite side dishes: easy, quick, full of peppery flavor and pairs fantastically with a number of protein recipes! Asparagus is a true power-food: It's a natural diuretic, detoxifier and source of fiber and inulin, which feeds your gut-friendly bacteria.

YIELD: 4 servings
PREPARATION TIME: 20 minutes

1 lb (454 g) fresh young asparagus

3 tbsp (45 ml) olive oil

½ tsp unrefined sea salt

¼ tsp freshly ground black pepper

Wash the asparagus, then trim about ½ inch (1 cm) off the bottoms. Pat dry with a towel.

In a large skillet, heat the olive oil, then add the asparagus. Season with salt and pepper, then sauté over high heat until asparagus is tender and just slightly browned, about 5 minutes. Serve hot.

NUTRITIONAL VALUES:

Total Calories:	Total Carbs:	Fat:	Protein:	Fiber:	Net Carbs:
441 kcal	16 g	43 g	11 g	11 g	5 g
Per portion	Per portion	Per portion	Per portion	Per portion	Per portion
110	4	10.7	2.7	2.7	1.2

SLOW COOKER RATATOUILLE

This recipe has more carbs than most ketogenic recipes, but it also provides a good amount of fiber, which is of vital importance for the health of your gut, and usually lacking in most Keto diets. It is a great, comforting side dish, blending the succulent flavors of eggplant and tomato.

YIELD: 8 portions
PREPARATION TIME: 20 minutes + 4 hours

1 medium eggplant

2 medium zucchini

½ tsp unrefined sea salt, plus more for sprinkling

1 small onion

4 cloves garlic

1 medium turnip, peeled

¼ cup (60 ml) white wine

3 tbsp (45 ml) olive oil

2 small tomatoes

2 tbsp (5 g) herbs de Provence

¼ tsp black pepper

Wash all of the vegetables. Cut the eggplant into ½-inch (1-cm) slices, then cut each slice into four quarters. Cut the zucchini in rounds.

Sprinkle the eggplant and zucchini with sea salt, then place in a colander and let drain for at least 15 minutes.

While the eggplant and zucchini are draining, chop the onion and the garlic, and cut the turnip into small cubes. Place the onion, garlic and turnip in the bottom of the slow cooker with the white wine and olive oil.

Chop the tomatoes, and add them to the slow cooker. Add the eggplant and zucchini, then the herbs, salt and pepper. Cook on high for 3 hours, then remove the lid, stir well and cook for another hour, or until the liquid has completely absorbed and the vegetables are cooked.

NUTRITIONAL VALUES:

Total Calories:	Total Carbs:	Fat:	Protein:	Fiber:	Net Carbs:
979 kcal	70 g	58 g	16 g	25 g	45 g
Per portion	Per portion	Per portion	Per portion	Per portion	Per portion
122.4	8.7	7.2	2	3.1	5.6

STIR-FRIED CHINESE LONG BEANS

Long beans can be a bit hard to find, but if you do find them you will become a fan of this humble vegetable. Long beans have great texture; they are firmer than a green bean but still tender, with a rich flavor that is well complemented by garlic. Long beans contain plenty of soluble and insoluble fibers and are a good source of vitamins C and A.

YIELD: 4 portions
PREPARATION TIME: 10 minutes

2 tbsp (28 g) coconut oil

2 tsp (6 g) minced garlic

1 lb (454 g) Chinese long beans, washed and trimmed to 3-inch (7-cm) lengths

¼ cup (60 ml) water

2 tbsp (30 ml) coconut aminos (see Note)

Melt the coconut oil in a large nonstick skillet or a wok over high heat. Add the garlic and stir until fragrant, about 15 seconds. Add the beans to the skillet and stir-fry for about 30 seconds. Add the water and coconut aminos, cover the skillet and let cook until the beans are tender, about 5 minutes. All the liquid should have evaporated, but if there is liquid remaining, uncover and cook for about another minute. Serve immediately.

NOTE: Coconut aminos are a great soy-free substitution for soy sauce. Find them in most health food stores or on the Internet.

NUTRITIONAL VALUES:

Total Calories:	Total Carbs:	Fat:	Protein:	Fiber:	Net Carbs:
495 kcal	47 g	30 g	15 g	12 g	35 g
Per portion	Per portion	Per portion	Per portion	Per portion	Per portion
123.7	11.7	7.5	3.7	3	8.7

VIVICA'S BIELER'S BROTH

Dr. Bieler (1893–1975) was an American physician who advocated food as medicine and author of *Food Is Your Best Medicine*. I am very much aligned with his theory of food as medicine; this is exactly what this book is about.

One of his most famous recipes is Bieler's broth, used for detoxification and adrenal and liver support. Because Bieler's broth is made with just vegetables, the carb content will be higher, but do not forget that fiber plays an important part here. In my version of his broth, I use bone broth as a base instead of water, then add the vegetables for nutrition. The broth is a great way to rebalance your sodium–potassium ratios, which is an important part of a healthy ketogenic adaptation.

If you are staying very strict with your carbs, remove the vegetables from the broth once cooked; if not, blend them together and enjoy the healing proprieties of this great recipe.

YIELD: 4 servings
PREPARATION TIME: 45 minutes

2 medium zucchini

½ lb (227 g) string beans, ends removed

2 ribs celery

2 cups (120 g) fresh parsley, finely chopped, divided

Fresh herbs, such as thyme or tarragon, tied together with a string, optional

1 quart (950 ml) homemade or store-bought bone broth (see Note)

4 tbsp (60 ml) olive oil

Put the zucchini, beans, celery, half of the parsley, herbs and bone broth in a medium saucepan and simmer until the vegetables are tender but not overcooked, about 20 minutes. When cooked, remove herb bundle.

Put the broth in a blender or puree it using an immersion blender, until a smooth puree is formed. Serve hot with a tablespoon (15 ml) of olive oil for each bowl and the rest of the parsley sprinkled on top.

NOTE: You can make bone broth by boiling marrow bones in a large stock pot of water for about 8 hours, then filtering.

NUTRITIONAL VALUES:

Total Calories:	Total Carbs:	Fat:	Protein:	Fiber:	Net Carbs:
857 kcal	33 g	58 g	29 g	15 g	18 g
Per portion 214.2	Per portion 8.2	Per portion 14.5	Per portion 7.2	Per portion 3.7	Per portion 4.5

CHICKEN CHICHARRÓNES

These "crackers" made of crispy chicken skins are almost better than pork rinds! I suggest that you eat them warm, for the best umami flavor, but you can drain them on a paper towel and let them cool to use as chips or crackers. They are great with guacamole!

YIELD: 6 servings
PREPARATION TIME: 20 minutes

6 chicken skins (from thighs and breast), about 2 oz (57 g) each

Preheat the oven to 350°F (177°C).

Lay the skins flat on a nonstick cookie sheet.

Bake until crispy and brown, about 15 minutes.

Consume hot or cold within 12 hours.

> NOTE: You can use the skin from the thighs you have used to make Slow Cooker Indian Butter Chicken (page 42). You can also buy skins on the Internet from meat retailers.

NUTRITIONAL VALUES:

Total Calories:	Total Carbs:	Fat:	Protein:	Fiber:	Net Carbs:
1021 kcal	0 g	91.5 g	45 g	0 g	0 g
Per portion	Per portion	Per portion	Per portion	Per portion	Per portion
255.5	0	22.8	11.2	0	0

BLT MEATBALLS

Do you miss the flavor of a BLT sandwich? This recipe re-creates it without the bad-for-you part: the bread! You can eat the meatballs by themselves with a side of green salad, wrap them in lettuce leaves or serve them inside a ketogenic bun! You can also serve them with a toothpick as an appetizer.

YIELD: 10 meatballs (10 servings)
PREPARATION TIME: 25 minutes

1 lb (454 g) ground beef, room temperature

¼ tsp dried thyme

¼ tsp dried herbs de Provence

½ tsp unrefined sea salt

½ tsp freshly ground black pepper

1 tbsp (14 g) butter, ghee or saved bacon fat

10 lactofermented dill pickle slices (see Note)

10 thin slices pancetta

10 cherry tomatoes

Preheat the oven to 400°F (204°C).

In a large bowl, place the ground beef, thyme, herbs de Provence, salt and pepper and mix well with your hands. Divide in half and form five meatballs from each half.

In a 12-inch (30-cm) skillet, melt the butter over high heat until almost browned, about 1 minute. Add the meatballs and sauté until brown on one side, about 2 minutes. Turn the meatballs and sauté another 2 minutes. Remove from the heat and set aside to cool for about 10 minutes.

When cool enough to handle, place a dill pickle slice on each meatball, then wrap in a slice of pancetta. Place the wrapped meatballs on a cookie sheet, together with the cherry tomatoes and bake for about 15 minutes.

Remove from the oven, and place a cherry tomato over each meatball before serving. You can use a toothpick to hold it in place.

NOTE: Lactofermented dill pickles can be found in most health food stores, in the refrigerated section.

NUTRITIONAL VALUES:

Total Calories:	Total Carbs:	Fat:	Protein:	Fiber:	Net Carbs:
1380 kcal	9 g	99 g	93 g	2 g	7 g
Per portion 138	Per portion 0.9	Per portion 9.9	Per portion 9.3	Per portion 0.2	Per portion 0.7

CRAB CAKES

Crab cakes are a classic restaurant favorite, so you might miss them when living the Keto lifestyle. This simple and tasty recipe, made with real crabmeat, contains no grains or artificial ingredients and can be made for a fabulous Sunday brunch . . . or for any occasion. You can use any leftovers for a quick weekday lunch on top of a salad or tucked in a wrap.

YIELD: 4 crab cakes
PREPARATION TIME: 15 minutes

½ lb (227 g) crabmeat

4 tbsp (60 ml) Keto Paleo Mayo (page 151)

½ cup (50 g) almond flour

1 egg, whisked until foamy

2 tbsp (8 g) fresh parsley, finely chopped

¼ tsp unrefined sea salt

¼ tsp black pepper

2 tbsp (28 g) butter

In a large bowl, combine the crabmeat, mayo, almond flour, egg, parsley, salt and pepper, mixing gently but evenly. Form into four patties.

In a large skillet, melt the butter over high heat. Cook the patties for 3 minutes on one side, then lower the heat to medium and cook for another 3 minutes.

Serve immediately. These are great with a Brown-Butter Salad (page 102).

NOTE: If you prefer, you can bake the crab cakes on a cookie sheet at 350°F (177°C) for about 25 minutes.

NUTRITIONAL VALUES:

Total Calories:	Total Carbs:	Fat:	Protein:	Fiber:	Net Carbs:
1431 kcal	12 g	131 g	61 g	4 g	8 g
Per portion	Per portion	Per portion	Per portion	Per portion	Per portion
357.7	3	32.7	15.3	1	2

SPICED NUT MIX

If you are tired of eating plain roasted nuts, this incredibly flavorful Spiced Nut Mix recipe will make your day! Hints of Indian and Middle Eastern spices will entertain your palate and provide antioxidant and anti-inflammatory properties. They are an easy snack to take with you anywhere. You can also use them as an appetizer or a snack to impress your dinner guests. Do not forget that nuts pack a calorie punch, so use small portions if you are trying to lose weight!

YIELD: 16 servings
PREPARATION TIME: 10 minutes

1 cup (125 g) macadamia nuts, unsalted

1 cup (120 g) pecans, unsalted

1 cup (150 g) almonds, unsalted

1 cup (130 g) walnuts, unsalted

½ tsp ground cardamom

½ tsp ground cumin

½ tsp ground coriander

¼ tsp ground cayenne

1 tsp unrefined sea salt

2 tbsp (28 g) butter

2 tbsp (24 g) LAKANTO® or erythritol (see page 168)

In a large skillet, dry roast the macadamias, pecans, almonds and walnuts until they are golden on the outside, about 3 minutes.

In a small saucepan, dry roast the cardamom, cumin, coriander, cayenne and salt, for about 30 seconds, being careful not to burn them. Add the butter and sweetener to the mix. Melt the butter and sweetener, stirring constantly until smooth and well blended with the spices.

Put the nuts in a large bowl and pour the spiced butter on top. Toss to coat evenly and let cool before enjoying. Can be stored in the refrigerator for up to a week.

NOTE: All nuts should be raw and unsalted. If you cannot find them, you can use roasted unsalted nuts.

NUTRITIONAL VALUES:

Total Calories:	Total Carbs:	Fat:	Protein:	Fiber:	Net Carbs:
3551 kcal	78 g	349 g	71 g	52 g	26 g
Per portion 221.9	Per portion 4.8	Per portion 21.8	Per portion 4.4	Per portion 3.3	Per portion 1.6

BREADS AND NOODLES

One of the biggest complaints I hear when people first start out on a ketogenic diet is that they miss bread. This is easy to understand if you've spent your whole life eating toast for breakfast and sandwiches for lunch!

I've put together a few uncomplicated and basic recipes to cover some of the varieties of bread you might miss. These breads might seem a bit odd at first, but after a few tries, they will become the new normal. You'll find them tasty and satisfying. More importantly, they provide many important nutrients and none of the problems associated with conventional bread!

ALL-PURPOSE KETO NOODLES

Sometimes I miss pasta! While I am not your typical Italian (I am not a huge pasta fanatic), there are moments when noodles can be a wonderful comfort food. Making healthy ketogenic noodles has been a bit of a holy grail of the Keto world. Most of the recipes out there are great, but they all contain some form of dairy. This recipe has no dairy and it is very rich in good protein and fiber. The texture resembles a good whole-grain noodle, and it can be used both with sauces and in a soup.

YIELD: 4 servings
PREPARATION TIME: 20 minutes

4 eggs

½ cup (40 g) super-fine psyllium fiber

½ cup (48 g) egg white protein (see Notes)

½ tsp salt

¼ tsp garlic powder, optional

In a large bowl, whisk the eggs lightly with an electric beater, then slowly add the dry ingredients, constantly mixing on low. Raise the speed to high and whisk until the eggs are well emulsified, about 1 minute. The dough will be wet and sticky.

Load the dough into a pastry syringe with a small round tip (about ¼ inch [6 mm] wide). If you don't have a pastry syringe, you can add the dough to a plastic zip top bag and snip off a corner with scissors.

Bring about 1 quart (1 L) of water to a boil in a 2-quart (1.8-L) saucepan. When the water reaches a rolling boil squeeze the dough into the pot, in a continuous stream. You will get one long noodle. If you prefer many individual noodles, cut the dough at the desired length when squeezing. Boil the noodles until fully cooked, about 1 minute. Drain in a colander. Use with your favorite Keto pasta sauce.

NOTES: Egg white protein can be found on the Internet, Amazon or Thrive Market, or in health food stores.

If you want to use the noodles in a noodle soup, squeeze dough directly into the boiling broth, boil for about a minute and serve.

NUTRITIONAL VALUES:

Total Calories:	Total Carbs:	Fat:	Protein:	Fiber:	Net Carbs:
566 kcal	51.2 g	19 g	141 g	48 g	2 g
Per portion 141.5	Per portion 12.8	Per portion 4.8	Per portion 35.2	Per portion 12	Per portion 0.5

CINNAMON SWIRL MUFFINS

This is a great variation on the classic cinnamon swirl bread . . . with none of the sugar or gluten!
You will love these muffins for breakfast or on the go.

YIELD: 8 muffins
PREPARATION TIME: 25 minutes

4 large eggs

½ cup (135 g) cashew butter

½ cup (50 g) crushed pecans

3 tbsp (36 g) LAKANTO® or
erythritol, divided (see page 168)

2 tsp (10 g) aluminum-free baking
powder

1 tsp ground cinnamon

1 tbsp (14 g) coconut oil, melted

Preheat the oven to 300°F (149°C).

In a food processor mix the eggs, cashew butter, pecans, 2 tablespoons
(24 g) of sweetener and baking powder until a smooth batter is
formed. In a small bowl, mix 1 tablespoon (12 g) of sweetener, cinnamon
and coconut oil until well blended, for the swirl.

Place 8 paper muffin cups in a muffin pan. Put about ½ teaspoon of the
swirl mixture in the bottom of every cup. Fill the cups evenly with the
batter, then pour another ½ teaspoon of swirl on top of the batter and
carefully swirl the batter with a toothpick.

Bake for about 15 minutes, or until a toothpick comes out clean from
the middle of a muffin. Do not overbake or the muffins will be dry.

NUTRITIONAL VALUES:

Total Calories:	Total Carbs:	Fat:	Protein:	Fiber:	Net Carbs:
1521 kcal	43 g	132 g	53 g	10 g	33 g
Per portion	Per portion	Per portion	Per portion	Per portion	Per portion
190	5.3	16.5	6.6	1.2	4.1

HERBED CROUTONS

These little croutons are a great add-on for almost any soup or salad. They can be stored at room temperature for up to a week in an airtight container.

YIELD: 10 servings
PREPARATION TIME: 20 minutes

Coconut oil, for greasing

4 eggs

1 cup (128 g) fine coconut flour

1 tbsp (3 g) fresh rosemary, very finely chopped

1 tbsp (3 g) fresh thyme, very finely chopped

½ tsp unrefined sea salt

Preheat the oven to 350°F (177°C). Grease a cookie sheet with coconut oil.

In a blender or food processor, mix the eggs, coconut flour, rosemary, thyme and salt to form a soft, runny dough. Spread the dough on the cookie sheet, about ⅓ inch (1 cm) thick, in a rectangular shape. Using a pizza cutter or a knife, score the dough to make 1-inch (2.5-cm) squares.

Bake until golden on top and fully cooked, about 15 minutes. Turn off the oven and let the croutons sit inside until fully cooled. Croutons should be hard and crunchy. If not hard, let them sit in the oven overnight. Remove from the baking sheet, break into pieces following the score marks and store in an airtight container for up to a week.

*See photo on page 126.

NUTRITIONAL VALUES:

Total Calories:	Total Carbs:	Fat:	Protein:	Fiber:	Net Carbs:
786 kcal	74 g	31 g	53 g	48 g	26 g
Per portion	Per portion	Per portion	Per portion	Per portion	Per portion
78.6	7.4	3.1	5.3	4.8	2.6

KETO ALMOND BUTTER BREAD

This is an all-purpose bread recipe that has a mild, smooth flavor. The texture is exactly the same as a loaf of regular bread, and it is great toasted as well.

YIELD: 10 servings
PREPARATION TIME: 45 minutes

Olive oil, for greasing

4 large eggs

½ cup (132 g) smooth almond butter

2 tbsp (24 g) LAKANTO® or erythritol (see page 168)

¾ cup (72 g) egg white protein (see Note)

2 tsp (8 g) aluminum-free baking powder

Preheat the oven to 300°F (149°C). Grease a loaf pan with olive oil.

In a large bowl, mix the eggs, almond butter and sweetener with an electric whisk, until smooth and foamy. Add the egg white protein and baking powder and continue whisking until the batter is smooth.

Pour into the loaf pan. Bake for 30 minutes, or until a toothpick comes out clean from the middle of the loaf. Do not overbake or the loaf will be dry.

NOTE: Egg white protein can be found on the Internet, Amazon or Thrive Market, or in in health food stores.

NUTRITIONAL VALUES:

Total Calories:	Total Carbs:	Fat:	Protein:	Fiber:	Net Carbs:
1240 kcal	30 g	84 g	100 g	16 g	14 g
Per portion	Per portion	Per portion	Per portion	Per portion	Per portion
124	3	8.4	10	1.6	1.4

KETO LARD BISCUITS

I am proud of how the "Keto-fying" of this classic recipe came out! Baking without gluten can be a real challenge, but in this recipe I managed to create a very similar result to the original biscuit. These biscuits are great for soaking up any sauce!

YIELD: 6 portions
PREPARATION TIME: 30 minutes

1 cup (128 g) fine coconut flour

½ cup (48 g) egg white protein
(see Notes)

1 tbsp (15 g) aluminum-free baking
powder

¼ tsp baking soda

½ tsp unrefined sea salt

6 tbsp (78 g) lard, very cold

1 cup (240 ml) fermented coconut
milk (see Notes)

Preheat the oven to 375°F (191°C).

In a large bowl, whisk together the coconut flour, egg white protein, baking powder, baking soda and salt. Add the cold lard to the bowl and using the tines of a fork, press it into the dry ingredients, until the texture resembles coarse meal. Add the fermented coconut milk to the bowl and quickly incorporate, without overmixing.

Place the dough on a cutting board, flatten with your hands into a disk, then cut out six biscuits with a drinking glass or cookie cutter about 3 inches (7 cm) wide.

Place the biscuits on a sheet pan, or in a springform pan close together, then put in the oven. Immediately raise the heat to 450°F (232°C), then bake until golden brown on top, about 10 to 12 minutes.

For best results, serve warm. These can be reheated in the oven.

NOTES: Egg white protein can be found on the Internet, Amazon or Thrive Market, or in in health food stores.

To ferment coconut milk, you can use a coconut yogurt starter, or you can use a teaspoon of probiotic powder. The probiotic mix must contain one or more of the following: *Lactobacillus acidophilus*, *Bifidobacterium lactis* and/or *Streptococcus thermophilus*. This is necessary for the sour "buttermilk" flavor.

NUTRITIONAL VALUES:

Total Calories:	Total Carbs:	Fat:	Protein:	Fiber:	Net Carbs:
1700 kcal	84 g	137 g	34 g	48 g	36 g
Per portion	Per portion	Per portion	Per portion	Per portion	Per portion
283.3	14	22	5.6	8	6

KETO NAAN BREAD TWO WAYS

This is an easy and basic flatbread that could be flavored in many ways. Try adding a bit of cumin or cayenne to the dough, or some herbs de Provence for a Mediterranean flavor.

YIELD: 8 portions
PREPARATION TIME: 30 minutes

1 cup (128 g) fine coconut flour

¼ cup (20 g) fine-ground psyllium husk (see Notes)

½ tsp garlic powder

¼ cup (24 g) egg white protein (see Notes)

1 tsp aluminum-free baking powder

1 tsp unrefined sea salt

⅓ cup (80 ml) melted coconut oil, plus more for frying or oiling

2½ cups (592 ml) boiling water

In a large bowl, mix the coconut flour, psyllium husk, garlic powder, egg white protein, baking powder and salt. Add the melted coconut oil and then the boiling water and mix well, until the dough starts to ball up. Let the dough rest for 5 minutes. When ready, it should be soft and pliable, like pizza dough.

Divide the dough into eight pieces, shape into balls, then one by one flatten into disks, about ¼ inch (6 mm) thick.

There are two cooking options for the naan.

To pan fry, heat about one teaspoon of coconut oil at a time in a nonstick skillet and fry the bread, turning once, until golden on both sides, about 3 to 4 minutes.

To bake, preheat the oven to 400°F (204°C). Lay the bread on an oiled cookie sheet and bake for 15 minutes, until golden and fully cooked.

For best results, serve warm. These can be reheated in the oven.

NOTES: Fine-ground psyllium husk and egg white protein can be found on the Internet, Amazon or Thrive Market, or in in health food stores.

If the dough is too runny, you can add more psyllium husk. If it's too hard, add a bit of hot water. Depending on the brand of your ingredients, the thickness of the dough can vary slightly.

NUTRITIONAL VALUES:

Total Calories:	Total Carbs:	Fat:	Protein:	Fiber:	Net Carbs:
2731 kcal	99 g	233 g	44 g	72 g	27 g
Per portion	*Per portion*	*Per portion*	*Per portion*	*Per portion*	*Per portion*
341.3	12.3	77.6	5.5	9	3.3

KETO SEED BAGELS

Bagels are a favorite, not only for breakfast or a snack, but for a tasty sandwich as well. You will love the rich flavor of these bagels and their versatility. They are also a great way to add fiber to your diet.

YIELD: 6 small bagels
PREPARATION TIME: 30 minutes

1 cup (112 g) coconut flour

½ cup (68 g) flax seeds, finely ground

1 cup (240 ml) boiling water

4 egg whites

½ cup (90 g) hemp hearts (see Note)

½ cup (75 g) sesame seeds

1 tbsp (5 g) aluminum-free baking powder

Sesame seeds or poppy seeds, for sprinkling

Preheat the oven to 350°F (177°C). Place a sheet of parchment paper on a cookie sheet.

In a large bowl, mix the coconut flour and flax seeds. Pour the boiling water over the flour and mix well, then set aside to rest.

Using an electric or manual whisk, in a medium bowl blend the egg whites until stiff peaks form.

Add the hemp hearts, sesame seeds and baking powder to the coconut flour mix and mix well.

Using an electric whisk or a wooden spoon, add the egg whites to the dry ingredients and mix well, without overmixing. The dough should still be somewhat crumbly but will stick together when formed into a ball.

Form the dough into six balls. Holding a ball in one hand, stick your thumb through it, making a hole, then place the dough on the cookie sheet and form it into a bagel shape, using your fingers. Sprinkle with some sesame seeds or poppy seeds so it looks pretty.

Bake for about 55 minutes, or until the bagels are golden on top and dry inside. You can use a wooden toothpick to check. It will be done when the toothpick comes out clean.

Let cool inside the oven for an extra-crunchy top.

NOTE: Hemp hearts can be found on the Internet, Amazon or Thrive Market, or in in health food stores.

NUTRITIONAL VALUES:

Total Calories:	Total Carbs:	Fat:	Protein:	Fiber:	Net Carbs:
1763 kcal	114 g	105 g	92 g	80 g	34 g
Per portion	Per portion	Per portion	Per portion	Per portion	Per portion
293.8	19	17.5	15.3	13.3	5.6

DRESSINGS AND MORE

A salad without a dressing is like a steak without seasoning. It's just flat and lifeless. Flavor is almost as important as nutrient content! These dressings are a great way to add important fats to your meals as well as add lots of flavor. I believe that every meal should be fun and enjoyable as well as nourishing and healing. These easy salad dressings and basic condiments will keep your taste buds entertained and your belly happy!

BUTTER LEMON SAUCE

This sauce only takes about 5 minutes to prepare, but it will surprise you with its bright, bittersweet flavor. It's a great sauce for any seafood, and it can be used on a salad as well. Feel free to be creative with it.

YIELD: 4 servings
PREPARATION TIME: 5 minutes

2 Meyer lemons

2 tbsp (28 g) butter

2 tbsp (28 ml) water

2 tbsp (24 g) LAKANTO®, erythritol or Swerve (see page 168)

Wash the lemons thoroughly, then cut into quarters and remove the seeds. Put the lemons in a blender and coarsely chop for about 30 seconds on slow speed.

In a small saucepan, melt the butter with the water and sweetener, mixing continuously with a spoon. When the butter is completely melted, turn on the blender and while it is running on slow speed, pour the butter mixture on top of the lemons. Turn the blender to high and blend until a very smooth puree is formed.

Serve immediately or refrigerate for up to a week. The sauce will thicken when refrigerated, but can be brought to room temperature to soften.

NUTRITIONAL VALUES:

Total Calories:	Total Carbs:	Fat:	Protein:	Fiber:	Net Carbs:
253 kcal	8 g	23 g	2 g	2 g	6 g
Per portion	Per portion	Per portion	Per portion	Per portion	Per portion
63.2	2	5.7	0.5	0.5	1.5

CREAMY AVOCADO DRESSING

This creamy, mild dressing is great on grilled fish or vegetables. Avocado contains health-promoting monounsaturated fats, especially oleic acid.

You can thin it out with some olive oil and make it into a salad dressing as well.

YIELD: 8 servings
PREPARATION TIME: 5 minutes

1 medium avocado

½ cup (120 g) coconut cream

½ tbsp (1 g) fresh cilantro, chopped

⅓ fresh serrano pepper (deseeded if you do not want it too spicy)

1 tsp fresh lemon juice

1 tsp unrefined sea salt

In a small food processor, mix the avocado, coconut cream, cilantro, pepper, lemon juice and salt on high until they form a smooth cream.

*See photo on page 140.

NUTRITIONAL VALUES:

Total Calories:	Total Carbs:	Fat:	Protein:	Fiber:	Net Carbs:
491 kcal	18 g	45 g	6 g	10 g	8 g
Per portion	Per portion	Per portion	Per portion	Per portion	Per portion
61.3	2.3	5.6	0.8	1.3	1

CREAMY TAHINI SAUCE

Tahini is made from iron-rich sesame seeds and is very popular in Middle Eastern and Mediterranean cuisines. Use it on a variety of grilled meats and as a salad dressing as well.

YIELD: 8 servings (1 tbsp [15 ml] per serving)
PREPARATION TIME: 5 minutes

¼ cup (63 g) tahini

½ cup (120 g) coconut cream

2 tbsp (30 ml) olive oil

1 clove garlic, pressed

½ tsp lemon zest

2 tbsp (30 ml) lemon juice

½ tsp unrefined sea salt

Mix the tahini, coconut cream, olive oil, garlic, lemon zest, lemon juice and sea salt with a whisk to make a smooth sauce.

NUTRITIONAL VALUES:

Total Calories:	Total Carbs:	Fat:	Protein:	Fiber:	Net Carbs:
1326 kcal	17.9 g	133 g	20.2 g	12 g	5.7 g
Per portion 165.7	Per portion 2.2	Per portion 16.6	Per portion 2.5	Per portion 1.5	Per portion 0.7

FERMENTED VEGETABLE JUICE

This drink is a powerhouse for your gut, and has more beneficial bacteria than
any probiotic in a capsule. It is also sour and refreshing; you can drink it as a daily health shot . . .
or serve on ice as a refreshing cocktail!

YIELD: 2 portions
PREPARATION TIME: 15 minutes

3 tbsp (45 g) unrefined sea salt

1 cup (240 ml) water, plus more to cover

2 cups (200 g) chopped celery

2 cups (200 g) chopped green beans

1 cup (120 g) chopped turnip or radishes

In a 2-quart (1.8-L) jar, mix the salt with the water. Close the jar and shake well until the salt is dissolved. Add the vegetables and cover with more water to fill.

Cover the jar with a paper towel and seal it with a rubber band. Let the jar sit on the counter for 5 to 7 days, depending on the temperature and the degree of fermentation you desire. After 2 or 3 days, the brew will start bubbling; that is a sign that fermentation has begun. You can taste the juice at that point; it should be bubbly and slightly sour. The longer you wait, the more sour it will become. I recommend storing it in the refrigerator when it reaches the desired level of sourness.

Strain to drink. The remaining vegetables are now also lactofermented and can be enjoyed as a side dish or condiment.

NOTES: It is important to use the best possible spring water you can find; do not use tap water, as it might contain too much chlorine, which kills the good bacteria.

For even more medicinal properties, you can ferment fresh ginger and turmeric together with your veggies (cut both into small chunks or grate before adding).

Because this is a ferment, the macronutrients for this recipe cannot be accurately calculated. I would consider it a "free pass."

GHEE

If you are trying to completely cut out dairy, using ghee instead of butter is a good alternative. Ghee is pure fat and it does not contain the dairy protein casein, which is one source of dairy sensitivities. This recipe shows you how you can easily make ghee yourself.

YIELD: 16 servings (1 tbsp [15 g] each)
PREPARATION TIME: 10 minutes

1½ cups (344 g) butter

Melt the butter in a small, heavy-bottomed saucepan over low heat for about 10 minutes. The butter will foam, then simmer, then eventually will form little brown bits at the bottom of the pan. Remove from the heat and strain through a fine sieve or colander.

Save the ghee in a glass jar. It can be stored at room temperature.

NUTRITIONAL VALUES:

Total Calories:	Total Carbs:	Fat:	Protein:	Fiber:	Net Carbs:
2150 kcal	0 g	240 g	0 g	0 g	0 g
Per portion	Per portion	Per portion	Per portion	Per portion	Per portion
134.3	0	15	0	0	0

KETO GODDESS DRESSING

This is my own ketogenic version of the famous goddess dressing, without the soy and hydrogenated oils. It contains plenty of healthy fats instead, and you will not be disappointed with the nutty and creamy flavor! This dressing can be used on salads or on your favorite Keto sandwich.

YIELD: 10 servings
PREPARATION TIME: 5 minutes

⅓ cup (84 g) well-stirred tahini (sesame seed butter)

¼ cup (60 ml) water

¼ cup (60 ml) fresh lemon juice

3 tbsp (45 ml) coconut aminos (see Note)

2 cloves garlic, pressed

5 drops toasted sesame oil

2 tbsp (30 ml) avocado oil

In a small food processor, mix the tahini, water, lemon juice, coconut aminos, garlic, sesame oil and avocado oil on high until a smooth cream forms.

NOTE : Coconut aminos are a great soy-free substitution for soy sauce. Find them in most health food stores or on the Internet.

NUTRITIONAL VALUES:

Total Calories:	Total Carbs:	Fat:	Protein:	Fiber:	Net Carbs:
1765 kcal	64 g	150 g	49 g	18 g	21 g
Per portion	Per portion	Per portion	Per portion	Per portion	Per portion
176.5	6.4	15	4.9	1.8	2.1

KETO PALEO MAYO

Mayonnaise is a great condiment for the Keto lifestyle. It is a versatile and tasty way to add nutritious fats to a protein-based dish. This recipe is super easy and can be easily doubled to make a bigger batch. The mayo will keep in the refrigerator for at least 10 days.

YIELD: 22 servings (serving size 1 tbsp [15 ml])
PREPARATION TIME: 5 minutes

1 egg plus 1 egg yolk at room temperature

½ tsp mustard

1 tbsp (15 ml) lemon juice

1 tbsp (15 ml) apple cider vinegar

¼ tsp unrefined sea salt or Himalayan salt

¼ tsp black pepper, finely ground

¼ cup (60 ml) MCT oil (see page 168)

¾ cup (177 ml) avocado oil

You can prepare this recipe with an immersion blender, a regular blender or a food processor. If using an immersion blender, layer all of the ingredients carefully in a large-mouth jar, starting with the egg, egg yolk and mustard, then slowly adding the lemon juice, vinegar, salt and pepper and finishing with the MCT and avocado oils. Lower the immersion blender all the way to the bottom of the jar. Without moving the blender, turn it on, on a slow setting, and run it until all the ingredients have blended together and mayonnaise has formed.

If using a blender or food processor, blend the egg, egg yolk, mustard, lemon juice, vinegar, salt and pepper until well combined. With the blender still running, add the oils in a very slow, thin, steady stream and blend until the mayo is thick and smooth.

NUTRITIONAL VALUES:

Total Calories:	Total Carbs:	Fat:	Protein:	Fiber:	Net Carbs:
3718 kcal	0 g	396 g	61.6 g	0 g	0 g
Per portion	Per portion	Per portion	Per portion	Per portion	Per portion
169	0	18	2.8	0	0

RED CURRY PASTE

This curry paste provides a bright and spicy burst of flavor. There may be some ingredients in the recipe that are hard to find, but once you have them this curry is easy to make and can be kept in the freezer for months. This paste can be very useful in a variety of recipes—with it you can instantly turn a bland dish into a flavorful one! This paste also combines many ingredients that are high in vitamins, minerals and antioxidants, making it a great medicinal food.

YIELD: 16 tbsp
PREPARATION TIME: 30 minutes

20 dried Thai chilies (2 inches [5 cm] long)

4 tsp (8 g) coriander seeds

2 tbsp (8 g) lemongrass, finely chopped

1 tsp whole peppercorns

1½ tbsp (10 g) grated fresh ginger

1 lime, zested

2 tbsp (2 g) fresh cilantro, finely chopped

4 tbsp (16 g) shallots, chopped

½ cup (70 g) fresh garlic, chopped

15 serrano peppers, deseeded and chopped

1 tbsp (5 g) dried shrimp powder (see Notes)

½ tsp sea salt

2 tbsp (30 ml) water

Soak the dried Thai chilies in a bowl of warm water until soft, at least 20 minutes, then drain. While the chilies are soaking, toast the coriander seeds in a dry skillet until fragrant, about 2 minutes.

Put the Thai chilies, coriander, lemongrass, peppercorns, ginger, lime zest, cilantro, shallots, garlic, serrano peppers, shrimp powder, salt and water in a small food processor and mix until a smooth paste forms.

NOTES: The paste can be frozen in an ice cube tray; when frozen, store the curry cubes in a zippered plastic bag in the freezer, to use individually.

Dried shrimp powder can be found in Mexican markets or on the Internet.

NUTRITIONAL VALUES:

Total Calories: 302 kcal	Total Carbs: 64 g	Fat: 3 g	Protein: 13 g	Fiber: 13 g	Net Carbs: 51 g
Per portion 18.8	Per portion 4	Per portion 0	Per portion 0.8	Per portion 0.8	Per portion 3

SPICY AFRICAN BUTTER

This fragrant spiced butter is a great fat add-on on to any plain meat or vegetable, creating an instant ketogenic recipe! It is also a medicinal food rich in vitamins and anti-inflammatory proprieties.

YIELD: 16 servings (1 tbsp [15 g]=1 serving)
PREPARATION TIME: 1 hour and 30 minutes

1½ cups (344 g) butter

1 small shallot, finely chopped

2 cloves garlic, pressed

1 tbsp (6 g) grated fresh ginger, or ginger paste

¼ tsp ground cardamom

¼ tsp ground cinnamon

¼ tsp ground cumin

¼ tsp ground turmeric

½ tsp dried oregano

In a small saucepan, melt the butter, then add the shallot, garlic, ginger, cardamom, cinnamon, cumin, turmeric and oregano. Cook over very low heat until brown specks start forming in the bottom of the pan, about 10 minutes, stirring often and making sure it does not burn.

Strain the butter through a fine mesh sieve lined with cheesecloth, into a clean jar.

The butter can be kept in the refrigerator for up to a month.

NUTRITIONAL VALUES:

Total Calories:	Total Carbs:	Fat:	Protein:	Fiber:	Net Carbs:
2423 kcal	4 g	264 g	0 g	0 g	0 g
Per portion	Per portion	Per portion	Per portion	Per portion	Per portion
151.4	0.2	16.5	0	0	0

SWEETS

Sweets should be just occasional treats, especially when dealing with insulin resistance and blood sugar imbalances. In this short list of recipes, I've distilled the best nourishing and healing ingredients, and just enough sweetness to warm your heart! Try the Healing Hot Chocolate (page 164) on a gray winter day and you will feel your body fill with warmth and energy!

BROWN-BUTTER COOKIES

These cookies will bring you back to your childhood. Simple and delicious,
they are full of good fats and fiber!

YIELD: 15 cookies
PREPARATION TIME: 20 minutes

½ cup (115 g) butter, unsalted

1 cup (100 g) blanched almond flour

½ cup (40 g) fine psyllium fiber

1½ tsp (6 g) aluminum-free baking powder

1 lemon, zested

½ cup (105 g) LAKANTO® or erythritol (see page 168)

1 egg, whisked until foamy

15 pecan halves

Preheat the oven to 350°F (177°C). Line a cookie sheet with parchment paper.

In a small saucepan, heat the butter over medium heat and cook until brown bits start to form at the bottom of the pan, about 8 minutes. Remove from the heat and let cool.

While the butter is cooling, mix the almond flour, psyllium fiber, baking powder and lemon zest in a large food processor.

When the butter is cool but still liquid, add the sweetener and stir until dissolved.

With the food processor running, add the butter to the flour mixture. Then add the egg in a slow and steady stream. A dough should form and come together in a ball.

Scoop 1 tablespoon (14 g) of dough out of the food processor, form it into a ball, then flatten it onto the parchment paper. Repeat until you have used up all the dough. Place a pecan half on each cookie. The dough should form 15 cookies.

Bake the cookies for about 10 minutes, until they are golden on top. Let them cool before removing from the parchment paper.

NUTRITIONAL VALUES:

Total Calories:	Total Carbs:	Fat:	Protein:	Fiber:	Net Carbs:
1779 kcal	59 g	161 g	32 g	43 g	16 g
Per portion 118.6	Per portion 3.9	Per portion 8.4	Per portion 10.7	Per portion 2.8	Per portion 1

CHOCOLATE HALVAH

Halvah is a soft dessert that is similar in texture to fudge. It's made with pure sesame paste and normally with honey or sugar. You will not be able to tell the difference with this sugar-free version!

YIELD: 24 servings
PREPARATION TIME: 20 minutes

¾ cup (161 g) LAKANTO® or erythritol (see page 168)

5 tbsp (60 ml) water

1½ cups (380 g) tahini (sesame seed butter)

Pinch of sea salt

2 oz (56 g) unsweetened dark chocolate

1 tbsp (15 ml) vanilla extract

Line an 8 x 8-inch (20 x 20-cm) baking dish with parchment paper.

In a small saucepan, mix the sweetener and the water and slowly heat until the temperature reaches 245°F (118°C), about 3 minutes.

In another small saucepan, over low heat bring the tahini and salt to 120°F (49°C).

In a small bowl placed in a larger bowl of hot water, melt the chocolate with the vanilla extract.

When the sweetener syrup is at the correct temperature, slowly add it to the tahini, in a slow and steady stream, mixing it slowly with a spatula. The mixture should not crumble and should reach a silky-smooth consistency.

Pour the tahini mixture into the prepared pan, then add the melted chocolate on top and carefully swirl in, if desired, using the back of a spoon or a chopstick. Do not overmix. Cool to room temperature, then refrigerate overnight to allow sugar crystals to form.

This can be stored in the refrigerator for up to a month.

NUTRITIONAL VALUES:

Total Calories:	Total Carbs:	Fat:	Protein:	Fiber:	Net Carbs:
6523 kcal	138 g	574 g	221 g	81 g	57 g
Per portion 271.8	Per portion 5.7	Per portion 23.9	Per portion 9.2	Per portion 3.3	Per portion 2.3

COCONUT CHOCOLATE BARS

Do you remember eating coconut candy bars as a kid? Those were the only candy bar I ever loved, so I had to re-create them with this recipe to fit my Keto Paleo lifestyle. I hope you will love this version as much as I do.

YIELD: 6 bars
PREPARATION TIME: 80 minutes

1 cup (75 g) unsweetened, shredded coconut

⅓ cup (80 g) coconut cream

1 tsp vanilla extract, divided

1 tbsp (12 g) LAKANTO® or erythritol, plus 1 tsp LAKANTO® or erythritol, powdered in a coffee grinder (see page 168), divided

2 oz (56 g) cocoa butter

2 tbsp (14 g) unsweetened cocoa powder

Line a cookie sheet with parchment paper.

In a medium bowl, mix the shredded coconut, coconut cream, ½ teaspoon vanilla extract and 1 tablespoon (12 g) of sweetener and blend well with a spatula or a spoon.

Place the shredded coconut mixture on the parchment paper. Using plastic wrap, shape the mixture into a flat rectangle about 4 x 6 inches (10 x 15 cm) and 1 inch (2.5 cm) thick (measurements may vary).

Place the mixture in the freezer for 2 hours, until frozen solid. Remove from the freezer and cut into 6 bars.

While the coconut mixture is freezing, melt the cocoa butter in a small saucepan until liquefied, about 1 minute. Add the cocoa powder, 1 teaspoon of powdered sweetener and ½ teaspoon of vanilla extract to the cocoa butter. Mix well over low heat for about 2 minutes, until all the ingredients are well blended. Let cool to room temperature, but still liquid.

Dip the frozen bars in the cocoa mixture, and turn to coat all sides evenly. Place the coated bars back on the cookie sheet and put in the refrigerator to harden, for at least 3 hours.

The bars can be kept in the fridge for a harder consistency or at room temperature for softer.

NUTRITIONAL VALUES:

Total Calories:	Total Carbs:	Fat:	Protein:	Fiber:	Net Carbs:
1492 kcal	43 g	151 g	12 g	18 g	25 g
Per portion 248.6	Per portion 7.1	Per portion 25	Per portion 2	Per portion 3	Per portion 4.1

HEALING HOT CHOCOLATE

Who does not dream of a delicious treat that is also healing to your body? This spicy and aromatic hot chocolate is anti-inflammatory and warming. It is perfect for long winter days when you need a treat, but can also really use an energy boost.

YIELD: 1 serving
PREPARATION TIME: 10 minutes

1 cup (240 ml) unsweetened almond milk

½ cup (120 ml) water

2 tbsp (14 g) raw cacao powder

½ tsp ground turmeric

½ tsp ground cinnamon

¼ tsp ground cayenne

1 tbsp (9 g) powdered gelatin

1 tbsp (12 g) LAKANTO® or erythritol (see page 168)

2 tbsp (28 g) coconut oil

In a small saucepan, heat the almond milk, water, cacao powder, turmeric, cinnamon, cayenne, gelatin, sweetener and coconut oil over medium heat, stirring constantly, until hot, about 2 minutes. Use an immersion blender in the saucepan to blend until the coconut oil is emulsified and foamy. Serve immediately.

NUTRITIONAL VALUES:

Total Calories:	Total Carbs:	Fat:	Protein:	Fiber:	Net Carbs:
260 kcal	7 g	18 g	14 g	5 g	2 g
Per portion	Per portion	Per portion	Per portion	Per portion	Per portion
260	7	18	14	5	2

KETO CASE STUDIES AND TESTIMONIALS

I would like to share a couple of patient case histories with you. This is to encourage you on your own journey and to give you some practical applications of the Keto lifestyle. These insights help show some of the results that can be obtained through adopting a Keto lifestyle and that these results are possible for you, too!

TESTIMONIAL FROM D.W.

D.W. was 57 years old and weighed just short of 300 pounds (136 kg). Her concerns were her elevated blood sugar and blood pressure, Hashimotos and hypothyroidism, chronic pain, fatigue, allergies, constipation, sleep disturbances and neuropathy in her feet.

When we started working together, she had been seeing a medical doctor and a chiropractor. She was feeling defeated and had lost hope in ever being able to lose weight and feel better.

After doing my program for eight weeks, she had lost more than 20 pounds (9 kg), and her blood sugars were back in normal ranges. Her blood pressure had also completely normalized, and she was able to stop her medication.

As we were working on supporting her digestion and balancing her hormones with the assistance of some supplements, eating the right foods was laying the foundation to enable weight loss without damaging her body further. She slept better and had more energy than she had experienced in 20 years. Here is what she had to say about it:

"Today I'm down two more pounds and have more energy than I have had in a very long time. My blood pressure has continued to be what it was in my twenties!! I am still taking [blood pressure medication] once a day, but if it stays this way another week, I'll start to decrease it a little at a time. A couple days ago I tried on a dress that I had grown out of . . . I'll be wearing it to my niece's wedding . . . ! It fits looser than it did when I wore it to my son's wedding about six years ago. It is so nice to feel good in my clothes! Thank you for all you've done to help me get on track to becoming healthy! I've been able to exercise more in the last two weeks than I have for over 25 years. I continue to do things that I thought at one time I wouldn't be able to ever do again!"

TESTIMONIAL FROM M.C.

M.C. didn't want to go through the same struggles as her husband in regards to losing weight. She was also experiencing imbalanced blood sugar levels, anxiety, depression, allergies and sleep disturbances. Her menstrual cycles were a mess and she experienced very low energy. She was on sleep, anxiety and allergy medications. Here are her results described in her own words:

"A HUGE thank you to Vivica Menegaz for all of her guidance and wisdom . . . My husband had gastric bypass in 2014 and lost 120 pounds (54 kg), but the last 30 pounds (13 kg) were not coming off. I didn't want to undergo surgery after seeing what he went through, and I was transitioning to eating all organic food and getting the toxins out of our home. One day at work, I was fed up and knew I had to get this weight off and hopefully get off my heavy dose of anxiety medications. The first few days were rough, but after day 4, I woke up with a lot of energy and [was] not starving. I was beyond excited!

Six months into this journey, I have [now] lost 54 pounds (24 kg). During this time I have had some dark moments dealing with some issues and going [off the Keto diet] two times. When this happened, I felt SO horrible with fatigue, anxiety, extreme hunger, etc. I had learned my lesson!

I'm not at my goal weight, but I am on my way there. My husband is now doing Keto and almost at his goal weight. This way of eating WORKS and I don't feel deprived of any foods like the other diets I have done. I am almost off my anxiety medications, and my goal is to slowly wean off them completely . . .

Trust Vivica and her program and get into the best health you can be! My husband and I have dealt with weight issues most of our adult lives, but now we are feeling better than ever, getting to healthy weights, our food bill has gone down considerably and I think we look better now than ever!"

RESOURCES

If you want to cook healthy recipes for yourself and your family, I recommend a few tools, which I use in my kitchen on a daily basis. They will make your life much easier.

SHARP CHEF'S KNIFE: Slicing meats and vegetables will become a pleasure instead of a chore when you invest in a good knife. All you need is one!

GARLIC PRESS: Instead of buying peeled garlic treated with chemicals, get fresh whole garlic. You do not have to peel the cloves to press them.

ZESTER: Citrus zest is not only full of vitamin C but also high in flavor-rich oils, without the carbs of citrus juice.

LEMON PRESS: This is a handy tool to squeeze lemons without getting the seeds in the juice. Also very easy to clean!

COFFEE GRINDER: I use it mainly to grind seeds and nuts on the spot, so they don't turn rancid if stored for long periods of time.

SMALL FOOD PROCESSOR: Ideal for quick, small batches.

LARGE FOOD PROCESSOR: A larger food processor is perfect for bigger quantities.

BLENDER: I recommend getting one with a glass cup so you can blend hot soups and your morning tea.

IMMERSION BLENDER: These are convenient for a number of jobs, like blending soups right in the pot, and are easy to clean.

MEASURING CUPS AND SPOONS: Decent measuring tools are necessary for any recipe.

DIGITAL KITCHEN SCALE: The scale is the most important tool to follow the recipes exactly.

LAKANTO® and erythritol are both natural sugar substitutes known to cause little or no insulin response when consumed, as sugar does. Both are readily available in health food stores, the health food section of most commercial grocery stores as well as online through Amazon or Thrive Market. LAKANTO® is a brand name sugar substitute that includes erythritol. Erythritol is something different, as is Swerve, and they are used for different purposes, usually regarding desired sweetness level.

MCT (medium chain triglyceride) oil is an oil that is commonly used in Keto cooking. It's available in health food stores or health food sections of commercial grocery markets. MCT is a source of healthy, more easily digestible fats.

ACKNOWLEDGMENTS

Writing my own cookbook has been my life dream since I was in my twenties! It used to be one of those big dreams that seemed completely unattainable.

Today, as I look at the pages of this book, I am still in disbelief. I could have never made this dream come true by myself.

First of all, I want to thank my mamma for allowing me to be born into the perfect environment. I spent much of the first four years of my life in the kitchen of a restaurant and around amazing chefs and foods. Thank you for letting me make a mess of the kitchen at age seven when cooking risotto with my best friend . . . It was our favorite dish! My mamma still supports me today, sending me books and magazines from Italy with inspiration for my work.

Next, I would like to thank my office manager and now dear friend, Patricia Woods. When things get crazy busy and life gets too overwhelming, she is always there with her calm and reassuring attitude and the skills to make everything work smoothly.

Huge thanks to Emily Uebergang. Her sharp intelligence and technical skills have rescued me more than enough times, and our relationship, starting as a blog collaboration, has bloomed into a great friendship and steady work together.

I would like to thank some of the most important people in my life: my clients and patients. They are the fuel that runs my engine. I am so grateful to constantly be witness to their amazing transformations, their courage and persistence every single day, and no matter how dire the situation, their will to live and heal. Thank you for being a constant inspiration to me, thank you for testing my recipes, thank you for following my advice and thank you for trusting me with your health! This book is for you; hopefully it will make your Keto life a bit more easy and fun.

Last but not least, a huge thank you to all the staff at Page Street, especially Elizabeth Seise, who accompanied me through the process of creating this book with great care and support. I could not have done it without you!

ABOUT THE AUTHOR

Vivica Menegaz is a certified whole-food nutritionist, blogger and one of the leading voices advocating for a food-based approach to healing.

She's also the founder of The Healing Foods Method—a fourteen-week online nutrition program in which she works one-on-one with clients to turn their health around utilizing a therapeutic Keto diet.

Tracing back to her Italian origins, Vivica is a passionate foodie whose love of healthy food has been shared with millions through her blog, The Nourished Caveman. As a former food photographer, she spent years immersed in the Los Angeles restaurant scene photographing (and eating) in some of the most incredible fine restaurants.

Transitioning to a life in Northern California enabled Vivica to pursue her self-sufficiency dreams and nutrition practice. Despite having adopted a Paleo approach to eating for many years, some nagging health problems began to crop up. It wasn't until one day when she decided to test her blood glucose levels that the rude awakening came: She was prediabetic.

Looking for answers, she stumbled across the ketogenic diet. It was love at first taste. Within the first few weeks, her blood glucose levels dropped, she shed excess weight, her brain-fog cleared up and her energy levels skyrocketed. She's witnessed this process repeated many times over with her clients through the work she now does in her private practice.

Combining this with her ancestral Mediterranean diet, and the Paleo diet she had used when first starting to study nutrition, she crafted her own template for eating. It's a therapeutic approach to eating that utilizes the healing power of foods to address the incapacitating symptoms of many degenerative diseases that have plagued our modern lives.

Vivica has made it her mission to help others reclaim their health and quality of life.

This cookbook is here to help you navigate your own Keto journey. Vivica will show you that better health is just around the corner and eating healthier is not as complicated, time consuming or expensive as you think.

Vivica is the co-author of *The Ultimate Paleo Cookbook* and the author of *The Everything Big Book of Fat Bombs*.

You can find Vivica's blog at www.thenourishedcaveman.com.

Her program is called The Healing Foods Method: www.thehealingfoodsmethod.com.

INDEX